From the
Geranium Farm

From the
Geranium Farm

A Second Crop of Daily eMails (112)
from
Barbara Cawthorne Crafton

CHURCH
Church Publishing Incorporated, New York

Library of Congress Cataloging-in-Publication Data

Crafton, Barbara Cawthorne.
     From the Geranium Farm : a second crop of daily emails / Barbara
     Cawthorne Crafton.
        p. cm.
     ISBN 0-89869-423-X
        1. Meditations. I. Title.

BV4832.2 .C685 2003
242—dc22

                                    2003058742

Church Publishing Incorporated
445 Fifth Avenue
New York, NY 10016

www.churchpublishing.org

5 4 3 2 1

In memory

of

Alexandra Palmer

1934–2003

The Spirit of 46th Street

Acknowledgments

Those most to be thanked for bringing about this second crop of Almost-Daily eMos are the thousands of people who read them, share them with their friends, respond to them. When navigating the computer's idiosyncrasies has become just about more than I can bear, the knowledge that people are waiting for these little essays makes me keep trying.

And then there is my family, those members with two legs and those with four, who cheerfully—or at least patiently—endure their appearances in my books. Blessings on them.

Still, the indefatigable Johnny Ross, editor from both heaven and hell by turns, is the one without whose energy, wit, good eye for detail, and deep love of our language this book would not sing.

The Players

Anna
Younger daughter of Barbara Crafton.

Community of the Holy Spirit
An Episcopal religious order for women. Barbara Crafton is an associate of the order, and practices spiritual direction in their convent in Manhattan.

Corinna
Elder daughter of Barbara Crafton.

Frances
Gardening buddy and writer. Actually farms on the Geranium Farm from time to time.

Gypsy
Formerly Rose's grey tiger tabby cat, now makes her home at the Geranium Farm. Protégé of What's-Her-Name.

HRH Genevra
Sometimes called "HRH," for short. Den Mother of the Geranium Farm, a title whose corresponding duties are vague at best.

Hummingbirds (Hummers)
Tiny birds native to North and Central America. Not found on the Geranium Farm, despite Barbara Crafton's desperate attempts to attract them.

Kate
Q's tortoiseshell cat. Highly critical of Barbara Crafton.

Madeline
Younger granddaughter of Barbara Crafton.

Q
Richard Quaintance, Barbara Crafton's English professor husband.

Rose
Elder granddaughter of Barbara Crafton.

What's-Her-Name
Well-known sociopathic calico cat of Barbara and Q.

Hope and Faith

"Let's stop at the bird place first," I say. We're on our way to the bird store and the grocery store. Unlike groceries, birdseed won't melt in the car. Besides, going to the bird store is a treat. I've always been something of an eat-dessert-first person.

"I need more of those sunflower seeds that don't make a mess," I tell the man who runs the bird store. But I am not looking at him. I am already gazing around the store at all the feeders and bat houses and birdbaths and bird books and birdhouses and a dozen different kinds of birdseed and gadgets to make squirrels quit bothering your feeder.

"You mean sunflower hearts," he says and brings out a big bag. "This is twenty-five pounds." The last twenty-five-pound bag we bought didn't last a month. Birds eat a lot.

"I want to get a bracket to hang a hummingbird feeder near the window where we can see them if they come," I tell Q, who is examining the bat houses. "Something that will let it hang a foot or two from the house. And I think we should get another hummingbird feeder."

Q looks pained. This summer of my obsession with hummingbirds has been a long one. "Don't you think we should wait until we see just one hummingbird?" he asks. Oh, please. Shouldn't I wait to start my degree until I already *have* a faculty appointment? Shouldn't I wait to begin exercise until I'm *already* strong? Shouldn't I wait to become an interesting, attractive person until I *have* a partner?

"No!" I say firmly. "They won't come if we don't show them we're ready. We have to have what they want *before* they come, or they won't come." I remind Q of his friend Pat, who has two hummers in her Metuchen yard. It can happen. I tell him about Margot, who waited two years before hummers came to her feeders. I mention that the hummingbird project is like evangelism in the church: you can't get new folks by doing only the things the old ones like. You have to do some new things, too. He says it's not quite the same thing. I tell him it's exactly the same thing, only for birds. I look to the bird store man for support. So does Q.

"Does anybody in Metuchen get hummingbirds?" Q asks the bird man.

"It can be hard to get them here," he says, with a frankness admirable in a man who makes a living selling birdfeeders. "But people in Metuchen do get them. South Brunswick, Somerville. They get a lot." He tells us about a person he knows who put a red balloon near her feeder—it bobbed around, and the hummers found it. I make a mental note: *Buy balloons.*

"You have to clean the feeders and change the nectar," the man reminds me. I do. I change and clean regularly. Q sighs. We come home with another feeder. He says he'll rig up a line to hang it from, so we can see it from the kitchen table. What a nice man.

You have to have faith. And more than a little patience. Moses and the Israelites wandered for forty days and forty nights before they reached the promised land. No, wait, it was forty years—*Noah* and his family were in the ark for forty days and forty nights until the rain stopped, and then a lot longer while they were waiting for dry land to reemerge.

I can see my hummingbird in my mind: I am at the breakfast table, and he comes to the feeder, hovering in the air while his long bill finds the sweet nectar in the garish red-and-yellow-plastic feeder. I know that my hummingbird may remain only in my mind—I may never really get one. But I do not tire of cleaning and filling the feeders for them, these hummers who may never come. For me, it is as if they were already here, as if I were safeguarding the health and well-being of bird guests I already knew. For me, it is like the food pantry at St. Clement's, my former parish in Manhattan: I wanted the food pantry to be full—always; that way, I knew we were ready for them. We have what hummers need—maybe not all of what they need, but some of it. They need what we have and they will come for it. We can be a part of their lives. In being ready for them, we are already with them in spirit. Even if they never come. They may not be in my garden, but they are in the world, and it is enough.

The preparation itself is part of the sweetness. Not just presence, but *anticipation* of presence. The Jews know this: they expect the Messiah, and prepare for the Messiah, and the Messiah has not yet come. And still they prepare. Again and again. And the songs they sing about their preparation are joyful songs. Because they *expect*. Their expectation has become part of who they are.

Soon the heavy heat will break. Soon it will rain. Soon we will awaken to the tiniest beginnings of a nip in the air, and soon the hummingbirds will begin to fly south. If a couple of them want to drop by for a snack, I'm ready.

Was Jesus Always Right?

I thought Phil seemed a little too enthusiastic. "THANKS FOR TAKING THIS SUNDAY!" he wrote in his big scrawl on the church bulletin he sent me. No problem, I thought, as I glanced through what I would be responsible for. "IT IS NICE (FOR ME) TO BE AWAY THIS SUNDAY," he scrawled at the top of the Gospel reading. I saw why: this week's Gospel is the one about the Canaanite woman who comes to Jesus asking him to heal her daughter who is possessed by demons, and Jesus says something really rude back. "I was sent only to the lost sheep of the house of Israel," he says first. Then the woman kneels before him and asks again, and he says "It is not fair to take the children's food and throw it to the dogs."

Ugh.

This is one of the Scripture passages that fall under the category "The Hard Sayings of Jesus," those recorded moments when he doesn't behave as we think he should. Who wants a Savior who acts like a New York waiter? Earnest church people have gone to great lengths to excuse such hard sayings or find a way around them—that Jesus didn't really mean it, that there was an obscure slang linkage between gentiles and dogs, so that this is really a commentary about first-century Judaism. We have a pretty rigid idea of what Jesus should and shouldn't do, and we'll do just about anything to protect it. We sing a cradle song at Christmas time about a baby Jesus who never cried. We hear of a runaway twelve-year-old, find him lecturing his elders in the temple, and refuse to scold him. We talk about a Jesus who "was in every way tempted as we are, yet did not sin." And we think this means he was without error.

But being without sin doesn't mean he never did anything incorrect. "Without sin" means that there was no separation from God. Jesus

---

4

was truly human and truly divine, we say. If so, surely part of being human is learning from your errors. You grow from your mistakes, and deepen from repentance. These things are our primary means of moral and spiritual learning, and Jesus—as both the Son of God and a human being—is meaningless if we strip him of them.

Why be afraid to take this story at face value? Jesus was mean to the woman and she called him on it. "Even the dogs eat the crumbs that fall from the master's table," she said. And he thought about what she said, and then he thought better of his actions and did something different. He allowed an old woman—and a Canaanite one, at that—to instruct him.

Who would I be if I had not seen my errors and learned from them? Who would I be if I were right all the time? Nobody of any use. I would be so far removed from human experience that anything I might say about it would be irrelevant. And who would Jesus be if his temptations were somehow less real than ours? His temptations were terrible—and they would get a lot worse than having a bad day and snapping at somebody.

It is never too late to do things differently. Correction can come from some pretty unexpected places, and we'd better be ready for it—if we want to become everything we can become. We should not be ashamed of error when it appears: shame cannot correct itself. It can only hide in silence, or stammer out a self-justification that doesn't hold water. Better to hear ourselves, and hear others, and have the guts to change.

This eMo, like several others in this book, was written on a Friday in anticipation of the Scripture readings specified in the lectionary for use on the following Sunday. The lectionary (see pp. 888–931 of the Book of Common Prayer) is a three-year cycle (Years A, B, and C) of scriptural readings that gives the regular worshiper a good overview of the entire Bible. This particular eMo, written in Year A of the three-year cycle, anticipates the Sunday in the church calendar known as Proper 15, for which the Gospel reading is Matthew 15:21–28.

The Cathedral

We swam through the clear water, looking down at the white sand as we went over it. So clean. Lit by the strong sun so that the sand sparkled even under the water's surface. Absolutely free of anything beyond itself. Savannah Bay on Virgin Gorda is a Caribbean postcard, a white arc of pristine sand edging turquoise water, surrounded by palms and sea grapes. On and out we swam, my little girls and I, but it was not the sunny swim over the clear sandy bottom for which we came. It was what lay beyond it.

In the distance, something dark: the sunny water ended abruptly ahead, and all was mysterious. Tall shadows, looming. Approaching the darkness, I felt a sudden foreboding. *You shouldn't take your children here. This is dark. Go back.* The dark place seemed to pull us toward it, as if we would be sucked into it and never escape. It grew taller as we approached. Perhaps we should turn back. Perhaps we shouldn't go any closer.

No. This is the sea. You know it well. There is nothing bad here. This is what you came for. Go forward.

And then we were there. And it wasn't really dark at all. It was the beginning of the reef. The first ancient arms of coral spreading in the water, and the first fish—creeping, nibbling, darting, nosing into little holes, disappearing into crevices and coming out again. Tiny black damsels with iridescent, electric blue sparkles that glowed in the dark. Red-eyed squirrelfish that poked quietly near the bottom at something tasty on a rock. Great parrotfish in psychedelic colors—fish with beaks! You could hear them pecking at the great corals. Flotillas of squid, steaming past in wedges like the wedges in which geese fly, turning all at once and jetting off in another direction. Strange exoskeletoned trunkfish, striped like zebras and triangular in shape, with pipelike noses and strangely intelligent eyes. Wary barracuda, minding their own business at the bottom and warning us without words to leave them alone. Motionless urchins, showing their spines among the corals: *DON'T TREAD ON ME.*

And the plants: funny flower ones that retracted suddenly into their holes when you went to touch them; tall green ones that waved in the current, stretching for the sun. And the corals, stony memorials to the billions of tiny animals whose bodies comprise them, whose completed lives still host the lives of other animals. Purple fan corals like undulating lace. Ancient brain corals hosting a score of small fish at once. Many-armed giant corals, like petrified cacti.

When we swam toward the reef, it was frightening. *I don't want to go there.* When we got there, it was beautiful, more beautiful than any bland expanse of clean sand could ever be. Sand is dead. The reef is alive, a community of souls, great and small, breathtaking in their individual beauties—a cathedral, taken as a whole.

A cathedral. The reef is like a cathedral. Weeks and years and centuries, layers of experience, eras of building and fallow eras, witness to countless lives, repository of destinies. The stone and glass souls of nameless craftsmen, alive still in the things they have left us, things whose origins are forgotten, whose meanings are forgotten or changed, whose wonder shines through the age and wear, the coral of human aspiration and skill.

And the people in it are very like the fish. Many of them, there from many places, for many reasons: intent on business, striding across the nave, kneeling in a chapel, gathering in groups to look and see, sweeping the floor, talking in pairs, hearing the organ, sitting in silence, thinking secret things, preaching public ones. The whisper of their presence remains in the cathedral after they are gone: long gone, or just gone. They lie in ashes in the columbarium. They stand in stone in the niches. Some were cut off in the prime of life, their names inscribed in a book eloquent in its heartache; others lie in dignity beneath their own effigies, dead from a gentle and dignified old age. The living light candles and weep, marry, and laugh. And the dead provide a place for them.

The great edifices of the natural world and the world of human creation are made of countless small lives. They are large, but they are not strange. They are ours. In them, life and death form a continuum. Life is not found in the uneventful swim over unblemished dead sand. It is found in the reef, that place that looked dark before we arrived there. When we arrived, it was lovely.

"You think about death too much," somebody said to me yesterday. I think about death *some*. We think death is dark. We are afraid. When we arrive there, we will find it is not so. I think we will find that it is alive.

Too Much Motet?

It's the radio announcer's birthday, and he gets to play anything he wants, he says. So he starts off with the Tallis Scholars doing a forty-voice motet. *Forty?* Good Lord. How many Tallis Scholars *are* there? They must have had to bring in temps.

Polyphony from composers like Thomas Tallis must have been terrifically exciting after all those centuries of music that barely moved. Two voices, three voices, four, eight voices interweaving with one another, becoming more and more unearthly as they climbed around each other—into the sky, like the Gothic cathedrals that were going up at the same time. Sublime.

Of course people wanted to add more and more. If eight voices is amazing, twelve will be *more* amazing. How about twenty? Human one-upmanship would inevitably come into play, and the goal would become the stuffing of voices into a short piece of music—like the way stuffing nuts and syrup between as many layers of phyllo as you can becomes the goal of baklava.

But music isn't baklava.

The motet started off well: one lovely tenor, joined by a treble. Then the organic interweaving began, more and more complex, lovelier and lovelier. *Ah,* I thought, and stretched under the covers as I lay and listened. As the voices piled on, though, it began to sound like one of those New York restaurants that caters to really hip people: crowded and noisy, like a gym. It ceased being music and became noise. There are limits to everything. A forty-voice motet is just too much motet.

It's so hard for me to admit that there can be too much of a good thing. Moderation has never been my strong suit. In the chapel at seminary, a thoughtful architect inlaid the seven fruits of the Spirit in beautiful ancient-looking letters right into the mosaic floor in front of the choir, where the students sat. He must have known we'd have trouble with some of them. My friend Denny and I used to sit as close to "Temperance" as we could, hoping that some of it would rub off on us. But it never did. Such moderation as we learned, we each learned later on, the hard way.

If one job is a good thing, three isn't necessarily better.

If one donut is delicious, that doesn't mean you should have six.

You don't double up a prescription drug on your own. You call your doctor.

That you *can* do something doesn't always mean you *should*.

"You know, we could put a feeder on the branch outside the bedroom window as well," I tell Q one evening. He doesn't think so. The feeders *are* getting a little out of hand. I think of the silence of the early mornings, of waiting for the first bird to sing in the almost-dark, my signal that it's okay to get up. I'm not sure exchanging that first sweet voice for the noisy arguments of twenty-nine gluttonous finches would be a smart trade.

Expecting Company

Today is the day the hummingbirds leave for Mexico.

I am ready to be their way station: the red plastic feeders are all cleaned and filled with fresh sugar syrup for one last time. Filled to the top, and overflowing—our well-trained ants began heading for them the moment I walked out the door. Each feeder location is marked with three or four bright red balloons, intended to attract nearsighted humming-birds, who will think they're flowers. I checked to be sure the balloons would be visible to someone who was flying by. The birdbaths have been cleaned and the water changed, in case they want a bath. Tiny cakes of soap and little towels ... no, just kidding.

"How do you know they'll start tomorrow?" I asked Genevra via email.

"Betty said," was her response. I don't know Betty, but if HRH Genevra does what Betty says, then this Betty must be somebody to reckon with. I'm going to believe her. And why not? Anybody who has entertained hummers is a better source than I am—I, who have entertained nary a one.

"How long does it take them to get here from upstate?" I typed.

"They should be there by about 2, assuming a westerly wind." Oh, for heaven's sake. She must think I'll believe anything.

Blowing up the balloons and cleaning the feeders and changing the birdbaths was fun. Imagining the hummers looking down from their flight and descending to the bobbing red orbs was enchanting.

In a Jewish home at Passover, a goblet of wine is placed at the festive table for Elijah. Some adult always makes sure it's surreptitiously emptied during the course of the meal: far into adolescence, the older children play along at believing Elijah really came, so the younger ones will believe. I used to do that for my kids about Santa Claus: he always ate the cookies and drank the milk we left him. And the Easter bunny always ate his carrot, leaving just the end behind, his teeth marks plainly visible in the hard orange flesh.

A mysterious, magical visitor. Someone for whom to prepare. Someone whose benign spirit will remember your remembering him and count it to you as righteousness. Someone powerful, who nonetheless needs a snack. Someone mightier than you, who nonetheless needs your help. And then disappears, leaving you only crumbs and an empty glass as evidence that he was there.

The singer Pat Boone (you remember him: the clean-cut singer whom people who boycotted Elvis liked instead) is one of those folks who scour the Bible for the exact day and time of the Second Coming. He ascertained that it would be on a certain day in October, and on that day, he and his family went outside in the yard and stood in a circle, holding hands, to wait for the rapture. They stood and waited. Waited. Waited. Eventually they went back inside, I suppose, and returned to their calculations.

Or maybe they did not. Maybe they went inside and talked far into the night, puzzling over what their disappointment might mean. What it might contain for them to use. Was it possible that Christ really had somehow come, and that his coming was not the thunderous event they had expected for years but something else? Was it possible that Christ was there with them at that moment, in their halting walk together out of disappointment with the past and into the future?

One hopes so, although I haven't heard, and this was years ago now. *I have a hard time with Jesus,* someone will say. *I don't feel close to him. I'm not even sure I believe in him.* But she knows that the earth is good, that love sometimes involves sacrifice, that worldly importance doesn't mean a damn thing, that the weak are specially deserving of care, that there is something greater in and under the universe than just us. She feels an eternal part of herself, something within her that cannot be separated from all that is, even by her own death. *Well, that's Jesus, I will tell her. Hold onto those things and stay tuned.*

Don't expect an attractive white guy in a long robe, who looks like everyone looked in 1968. Don't expect any specific thing. Just expect.

Meanwhile, I believe hummers will visit me—which means that in some sense they already do.

What Power Really Looks Like

There is a persistent and incorrect myth about hummingbirds: that they hitch a ride south on the backs of migrating geese. What an ugly rumor. Vicki gave me a little book about hummers with a whole page dedicated to debunking myths about them, and this was the first one. They don't ride geese down to Central America. They fly there themselves.

I can understand how such a belief must have started. Hummers are so small! They're less than three inches long and they weigh about as much as a business letter. How could something so little fly thousands of miles? It can't be. They *must* attach themselves to big strong geese.

One of the other myths is that you have to stop feeding them or they won't migrate. Not true, either. They know when to go, and they go when it's time.

These myths reveal more about us than about the little birds. It is not they who doubt their ability because of their tiny size. We are the ones who can't imagine self-sufficiency in companionship with smallness. We keep looking for the mighty. You have to be big and strong. Important. Visibly powerful. But you don't have to be big or visibly powerful. All you have to be is tough and persistent.

We have a hard time accepting this as a possibility. Take the tired old anti-Shakespeare myths, for instance: that the obscure commoner from Stratford-on-Avon couldn't possibly have written those plays, that it must have been a nobleman, someone with much more heft in the world, someone whose schooling was more respectable, someone more credentialed. We can't get our minds around the idea that a genius may have arisen from outside the normal channels of greatness.

Small people aren't supposed to have power or authority. Simple people aren't supposed to do important things. They should be left to important people. But small people have the power they choose to claim and exercise. And there are no simple people. Some of us are just quiet.

Look at a baby learning to climb the stairs. He holds your hand and up he goes. The stairstep comes up to his hip, but he lifts his leg and makes the step. You are amazed at how little support you had to give him—he really did do it by himself. You imagine yourself trying to step up on something as high as your hip, and you get sore just thinking about it. *How does he do that?* you wonder.

He can do it because he claims his power and summons it. And because it is time. He can do something that looks to be clearly beyond his strength and size. You watch him and realize that strength and size aren't the same thing.

And forget cats. They see something of interest up on a shelf somewhere up near the ceiling and, in a leap, they are there. A leap, in one bound, to a point six or eight times their height. You imagine yourself gathering yourself and springing up, and you know that you'd be lucky to make it to the chair seat.

There's power and then there's power. Not all power looks as we think it should. God seems to have given us the power to do what we need to do—not always what we think we need to do, but what is really necessary. You can't leap up to a shelf near the ceiling because you don't need to. You can get a stool and reach up there to get what you want.

But you can do the things before you that need doing *by you.* You're not Superman or Wonder Woman, and you don't have to be. You're a human being, with a lot more power than you think.

This Old House

"Guess where we went today?" asked my daughter Anna on the phone. She and her boyfriend had just returned from a trip to Atlanta by car.

I puzzled for a moment. "Where?"

"Forest Hill."

"No! Did you see Granddad's house?"

"Yes. You'll never guess what it is now."

My heart sank. A Tastee Freeze? Part of a strip mall? Torn down to make room for a McMansion?

"What?"

"It's a bed-and-breakfast. It's called 'Be My Guest.' There's a cute sign out front."

"No!"

"Yes! It's really cute."

It's grey now, instead of the yellow it was when we lived there. She didn't recognize it at first because of that, until she saw the little barn.

So the little barn is still there. *Anna, tiny, venturing carefully into the darkness of the barn to bring her grandmother a potato and emerging with it, flushed with pride at her own courageous act, the dusty root clutched in her little hand.*

The garden is still lovely. *My father, setting up a tree stump as a stool for my mother to sit on, so she could watch him work in the garden at the end of her life.*

The field behind the house is no more: rows of new houses come right up to the fence now. *You could look across it long ago to a wood and the hills half a mile away; the sun set over them each day and slanted lovely, sad light into the yard, deepening slowly into the shadows of twilight.*

The big trees are still there. *Corinna, three years old, waving to me from a branch outside the second-story window. "Come down from there," I said, frightened, and watched her climb efficiently down.*

The awning on the back window is gone. It came from Grove's Store, bought by my father when the little store closed down, vanquished by the mightier Klein's Store across the road in what was definitely a one-store town. *Poor Mr. Grove, staring morosely out his window in his quiet store at the brisk traffic across the way.*

The music room is now a living room. *Me, sitting at the piano bench in the afternoon, getting it wrong and getting it right, over and over again.*

That's a small house for a bed-and-breakfast. I can't think there's much money in it. Maybe it's something of a retirement hobby. But somebody saw how lovely our little old house was, and wanted to share it. The town is no longer tiny. The houses come right up to the fence in back. But a piece of the past remains.

The Fullness of Time

Q groped for the Italian word to describe the condition of the fruit we hoped to have for dessert. "Here you never serve the fruit hard, or cold," he said. "You wait until it is...," he gestured with his hands, a small but eloquent rolling motion beginning at the breast and ending with palms raised toward the generous benediction of heaven, and raised his eyebrows inquiringly.

"...*morbida*," the waiter said obligingly.

Morbida. Literally, "about to die." In Italy, where there is simply no such thing as a bad meal, there is also no vernacular term that would translate into English as "shelf life." You eat it fresh and local there, or you don't eat it. And you eat it when it's ready to be eaten, and not before. You eat it when it's *morbida*, when not a moment is left in which to ripen, fully fragrant, full of its own sweet juices, as soft as it's going to get before it starts downhill toward decay. You don't arrest it before it can reach that state, embalm it in icy air for weeks on end and then bite into it when it's hard enough to break a tooth and all the taste has been chilled right out of it. No. You watch it and smell it and feel it and wait. Until it is *morbida.* Fruit is at its most perfect when it is about to die.

Its mission is to die. Fruit surrounds the seed in order to tempt animals—like us—to pick it and eat it and drop the seed somewhere. If enough animals eat enough fruit and drop enough seeds, there will be an ongoing supply of new fruit trees and plants, and they will be in new places—wherever the animal took the fruit it was eating. This is the goal, as far as the plant is concerned: to reproduce itself and extend its range.

The fruit doesn't mind. Its work is done. Two juicy fat yellow peaches arrive in a bowl of water. *We who are about to die salute you,* they say. *Hey, no problem,* I answer, and cut through the downy skin into the sweet yellow pulp for the first bite.

It lives, too, of course, before its work is done. It provides beauty and color—self-interest on its part, as it wants to attract transportation, but a delight to us. It provides a wonderful smell as it ripens. Fruit causes poetry and song among its human admirers, and we think it so lovely that we paint pictures of it and hang them on our walls. It contains enough electrical energy within its pulp to power a clock (truth: I used to have a clock that used an orange as its battery). It nourishes other species of living things, and whatever is left over rots and enriches the soil.

We think death is a defeat. We view it as our great enemy, and try at all costs to keep it as far from us as possible for as long as possible. This makes sense: it is not time for us to fulfill our season here until we are *morbida,* until we are ripe, until we have become as good as we're going to get. Until we are ready to die. That is why early death unsettles us so, and plunges us into a raw sorrow quite unlike the august grief we feel when one of us dies at a venerable old age, grief so mixed with gratitude for a long life well lived that it almost doesn't hurt. Early death has no sweetness for us.

But a life that ended in an early death is not futile. It was not meaningless because it was short. The fruit eaten before its time still carries the seed and plants it. The human life ended before it has become all it would have become still carries the firm pulp of our love all around its precious kernel, firm and clinging, protective, and that love can still nourish something. It is tossed rudely to the ground before it can fall there. But it will do its work even so, slowly, finding its way to become part of the earth from which it came and to which it is not strange. They become nourishment to us even though they left us and returned to earth too soon. We feel that nourishment. We are better because they were here with us, if only for a shortened time.

They eventually go home, too, as we are going home. We all go home.

Only Love Lasts

"Please swipe card again," it says on the subway turnstile. Okay: you take your MetroCard and run it firmly down the long slot, and this time it works: it not only tells you to go ahead but also how much money you have left on your card. New York sure has changed: that's not what "swipe" used to mean here at all.

"Did we have MetroCard when you left?" I ask, "I can't remember when it started."

"Yeah," Cynthia says, "it had just gotten into all the stations."

Cynthia moved from New York to Houston three years ago, and this is her first visit back. We're catching up: where she's going to go while she's here, who she's going to see. Whether she's going to go down to the World Trade Center site—yes, absolutely, coming in on the plane was so strange without the towers, you couldn't tell what city it was, but then she saw the Chrysler building, and she was oriented. She's going to Yankee stadium on Tuesday afternoon: she doesn't really have a favorite team anymore, she says: anyone's fine, as long as Dallas loses. Then she's going to the Cathedral of St. John the Divine on Wednesday evening for the memorial service: Richie Havens is playing, and Jason Robert Brown, I think, and, tucked in among all those luminaries, I'm going to read an eMo.

I'm glad to be going there. For weeks I've been dreading the 11th of September. Tiptoeing away from the drumbeat of coverage on the television. Not wanting to think about what the pile was like, hating the sight of my hardhat on top of the armoire but unable to move it. Hit squarely in the solar plexus by the two-page spread of the final list of names in the *Times*: so long, so bald, scanning down the columns to see if the people I knew were there and shocked all over again to see that they were.

Then yesterday I managed to listen to the "Sonic Memorial" on WNYC. All about the buildings, and what went on there: recordings of how the elevators sounded—remember that long *whoosh*?—and how the revolving doors sounded; interviews with couples who were married there, people who worked there, the engineers who made it run. I could finally hear a cellphone call from a man on one of the planes telling his wife that he absolutely loved her. "I absolutely love you," he said. "Tell my parents I absolutely love them, too."

I absolutely love you. Love is the only thing that really is absolute. It's the only thing that endures. Buildings don't. Subway tokens don't. People don't. But the love they shared does. "Let us love one another," it says in the letter of John, "because love is of God." We read it at weddings. We ought to read it at funerals, to celebrate the thing we do that is most like what God does, the thing we do that, alone, survives us.

Flag Etiquette

It's the first anniversary of the attack. I am out on the porch putting up the flag. Q fixed a bracket to one of the pillars, so it's easy to put it up. We don't fly it every day. Just national holidays. Its flagpole is a piece of bamboo from the back yard; the old flagpole broke.

This flag is very brightly colored, and very colorfast. It's made of nylon. I still have our old forty-eight-star flag from when I was a girl. That flag is very heavy, coarse cotton. It's a little on the faded side. My father used to fly it on national holidays, too. Towards the end of his life, he flew it every day—not the old forty-eight, but a shiny new fifty like the one we have today. It's not flag etiquette to fly an earlier version of the flag.

Flag etiquette. With all the flag-waving that goes on these days, the manner in which the American flag is treated is distressing to someone schooled in flag etiquette. You don't fly it when it rains. You take it down at sunset. You don't fly a tattered flag, you replace it; and you don't just throw the old one away, you burn it. If you put a flag up somewhere, you're responsible for seeing that it remains in good shape; you don't just slap it on a bridge in September, spray-paint "These Colors Don't Run" next to it and then walk away, leaving it to be buffeted and torn to shreds by the wind and rain until it's an unrecognizable rag by April. You don't make windsocks and sweatshirts and beer can holders and car ads out of it, either. Some of us remember when Abbie Hoffman went to jail for wearing a shirt made out of the American flag. I'm not sure the punishment fit the crime there, but still: you don't just slap it on any old thing. You *fly* it.

Immediately after the bombing of the World Trade Center, car flags appeared everywhere. I was accustomed to seeing small American flags only on government vehicles; for a week or two, it felt like the president was in town wherever you went. Only it was always just a mom and two toddlers or a guy in an NYPD baseball cap.

I suppose flag etiquette can change, like everything else. We have worse problems as a nation than American-flag beer can holders. We have a strange war, a war that doesn't feel like a war. We have fear about another attack. And we have a year's worth of sorrow—sorrow that feels fresh today, feels newer than it is.

I turn to go back inside, and two mourning doves begin to sing. One calls to another and the other answers, a low note rising higher, and then three low notes. A quiet call, quiet and a little sad, to my ears. Probably not to theirs, though. However much we may anthropomorphize our cats and dogs, our emotions are not shared by the animals. To us, the song of the mourning dove is about love and loss. To them, it's about territory or mating. Life goes on.

"I just want it to be over," a young woman tells me. "I don't want to see it on television, don't want to go to a church service, don't want to do anything. I want it to be over."

Mourning in the nineteenth century was a very orderly process. It was conducted in stages, and each stage had a prescribed manner of dress: veiled, with black clothing and jewelry; then unveiled, with black clothing and jewelry of any color; and then banded—a black ribbon worn around the upper arm. It advertised that the person was a person in pain, warned others to be gentle with her, not to expect too much.

You were excused from social obligations, like calling on people in their homes. You were excused for an entire year. You had to play your part. There were certain activities in which a mourner didn't engage; think of Scarlett O'Hara dancing at a party in her mourning clothes, and the stir it caused among the other guests. Mourning didn't just protect you:

it also prescribed exactly how long it was supposed to take you to recover. Not sooner, and not later. And when it was over, it was supposed to be over.

It's the *over* part, then and now, that doesn't work for human beings. History doesn't un-happen. We don't get the dead back. We never again get to be the people who have not yet had this loss. We heal up as best we can and get back to work as soon as we can. But we will always have had it: stylized and formulaic, like mourning in the nineteenth century, or impatient and pell-mell, like our own. The human race always has mourning to do. And life always goes on, too.

How are we doing? We're doing beautifully. Sad, but why wouldn't we be sad? Mad? That, too. Scared? You'd be a fool not to be. Paralyzed? Not on your life.

The manor house of the Geranium Farm is four shades of purple, and the underside of the porch roof is sky blue. The flowers out front are not arranged in Gertrude-Jekyll-style, elegant drifts, but in eccentric stands of individual plants, chosen either because I just like them or because I think they'll attract hummingbirds. There are probably too many bird feeders. The Geranium Farm looks like the Garden of Eden on amphetamines.

And Old Glory waves in the breeze off one of the porch pillars. He doesn't harmonize with anything, either. He doesn't need to. He's got his hands full just waving.

Harmony isn't everything. It isn't even very real. Nature isn't about harmony, and neither is life. Nothing ever really resolves. There's no such thing as "closure" if closure means it's over. "Closure" just means it's happened, and that we know it. That it's in our lives now, along with everything else. And that life goes on.

Vengeance Isn't Mine

This is hard for us this September. We're still bruised from last September, a year after the World Trade Center was destroyed. Forgiveness is far from many hearts. If we are honest, though, we must admit that it isn't really only this year and our terrible national sorrow that makes forgiveness hard: it's always been something we don't do well. We've *never* been good at it. It's not just Osama we can't forgive; we still haven't forgiven our next-door neighbor or the girl who was so mean to us in junior high or our former husband or wife. I was leading forgiveness retreats long before 9/11.

I wander the country frequently to help congregations and dioceses think together about matters of the spirit. Of all the things that might conceivably come under that heading, forgiveness is the one we most frequently discuss, since I have noticed that many, many people find it a difficult and painful subject. *My old anger inhibits my prayer and meditation ... I can't forgive him: I'm too angry ... She doesn't deserve forgiveness after what she did ... I can't forgive him: I'm still too scared of him ... After all these years, I still can't forgive myself.*

One of the things we do when I am leading a forgiveness retreat is develop a list of things forgiveness is and is not. It takes us a whole day to discuss each item on the list, but I offer them to you today. Perhaps they will begin some useful thinking of your own.

☐ **Forgiveness is not acquittal.** It doesn't mean the person is innocent. If he were innocent, forgiveness wouldn't be required. You only forgive the guilty. Forgiveness is not saying "It's okay." We don't have to forgive things that are okay. Forgiveness is only for things that *aren't* okay.

☐ **Forgiveness does not mean there are not consequences to human action.** God may forgive one convicted of a crime, but he still must serve his jail sentence. Our actions and their consequences are part of history, and so is our punishment. Forgiveness is not about letting people off.

☐ **Forgiveness is not a feeling.** It is a theological decision. If we had to wait for a great rush of warm, fuzzy feelings about someone who's hurt us terribly, we'd be in for a long wait. Feelings may lag far behind the theological decision to forgive, and they typically do. But the decision can be made in advance of them. It is really a decision to turn a problem too hard for me over to God, who can handle it. Once I have decided to do that, I can say I have forgiven, and wait in patience and hope for God to complete more and more of the healing of the hurt and anger that have gripped me.

☐ **Forgiveness is actually more about me than about the one I forgive.** It is about freeing myself from that to which I cling, setting myself free from my bondage to an old injury, freeing up space in my heart better used for another purpose. In this process, the one I forgive also becomes, in my mind, more than simply his offense against me.

☐ **Forgiveness is really not about the past.** It's not an opening and reopening of the case against the accused. It's about closing the case, once and for all, and walking freely into the future, rather than endlessly circling the past. Forgiveness is never to be found in the past. It can be found only in the present and the future.

These are the main things that develop as we talk together, and they seem to be pretty much the same for people wherever I go. Some of them are hard for hurting people to swallow at first, but much of the spiritual life is hard at first, and nobody ever said you develop one in a day.

If you would like to read more about forgiveness, here are two books that might be helpful: my own, *Yes! We'll Gather at the River* (Church Publishing, 2001), and L. William Countryman's *Forgiven and Forgiving* (Morehouse, 1998).

Beach Walk

The beach was smooth as silk, sprinkled with delicate little shells dropped there in the night by the sea. The fishing boats had been out for hours, but pedestrians were few and far between, and it was already almost time for them to disappear. It's hot on the beach in Florida unless you're in the water. I think you don't walk there except in the early morning; once the sun is up, it's time to go inside.

As Patti and I walked along the sand, she told me that alligators are actually seen in salt water sometimes. Alligators!

"Yes, Norman saw one once, while he was fishing right from here" she said. "As a matter of fact," she went on encouragingly, "it began to head for the shore."

"What did he do?"

"He just kept walking slowly parallel to the water," Patti said. "You're not going to outrun one of them."

I see. Norman is a runner. If he can't outrun an alligator, I sure can't.

"Where is Cuba?" I asked, shading my eyes with my hand. "It must be right out there."

"Yes, right over that way." She pointed to the horizon.

"It was scary here in 1962," she said.

It was scary everywhere in 1962: everyone during the Cold War thought the bomb was going to fall directly on his living room, but people in Florida had the unhappy distinction of knowing that, in their case, it really would. Patti's part of Florida is an immense military area, the closest one to the guns of that long-ago October. Soviet missile launchers were trained on her and her family.

You just walk very slowly parallel to the water, and the alligator thinks you're not a threat.

In 1962, our young president had already learned the hard way that you don't rush an alligator. The disastrous Bay of Pigs invasion was still fresh in our memories. We studied the grainy newspaper photographs of what looked to be Cuban missile-launching sites, taken by our guys flying overhead, and wondered what he would do now. And then he went on television and told us: we would surround the island with a naval blockade until the missiles were gone, and we would respond to these clear signs of aggression from the tiny outpost of Soviet power with any means at our disposal, including nuclear weapons.

You just walk parallel to the water, and the alligator knows you're about his size and may be as strong as he is.

Alligators from the sea. Missiles trained on our shores. The whole point of the Cold War was that we would all choose our battles, and that we wouldn't choose one that might kill us all. For forty years it worked, sort of: the world forgot almost completely what peace of mind was, but at least we didn't all die.

Of course, it may be that the world has never known what peace of mind is. Every age has been violent in its own way. Nature is violent in its way. To a visitor from another planet, our behavior probably looks little different from that of the alligator: we're aggressive, watching each other suspiciously all the time, apt to attack, only holding back if we think we won't win. As a race, we've never lived in any other way for very long. Our wars are the primary bookmarks of our history texts.

And yet we dream of peace. We imagine that we prefer it, and in our dreams, we convince ourselves. Every society describes itself as peace-loving. Every aggressor identifies himself as acting in self-defense. And when we are invaded, our dreams of peace intensify in their sweetness: we think our country most beautiful when it is in danger. This love feels pure to us: pure and so strong that some of us are willing to die for its sake. And some are willing to kill.

I wonder if our dream of peace is only a dream. If that's all it can ever be. There was a time when people thought that our technological skill would propel us into a world of peace and progress. Nobody who survived the twentieth century could possibly think that anymore. All technology did was give us more efficient ways of killing.

The great eras of mysticism have always coincided with eras of political and social unrest. The fourteenth century was one such era; the decades surrounding the collapse of the Roman Empire was another. Jesus' own era was another. When our confidence in our own strength is shaken, we turn to another strength. When we think death is near, we think of heaven. When we are battered by war, we reach for the peace of God.

"Here there is no enduring city," wrote St. Augustine as the Eternal City crumbled and the world as he knew it ended. If there is a gift to our era of fear, it is this: it can turn us in the direction of the God who alone is our hope if we will allow ourselves to be turned there.

You walk slowly parallel to the water. The alligator does or does not come ashore. You do or do not outfight him. You will not outrun him. But you walk slowly parallel to the water.

Eyes on the Prize

I have to row 100,000 meters by October 15th.

Well, I don't *have* to. But I want to. I've entered a contest, and there's a prize if you get to 100,000. This presses some buttons. *Contest? Prize? Where?*

I figure if I do 5,000 five times a week, I'm there. I haven't rowed yet this week. So I may need to do 6,000 each day. The backs of my legs begin to ache a little when I hit 3,000, and by the time I hit 5,000, I know it.

I know what will help.

I am the only woman in the galley. "We keep you alive to serve the ship," says the overseer, cracking his whip. *No, cookie, the ship is keeping me alive,* I think as I feel my arms and shoulder muscles work and my heart beat.

I row with a hundred other rowers up the Nile. We power Cleopatra's barge. Three or four Roman generals follow us in their galleys, as fast as they can, the poor guys at the oars pulling for all they're worth: Cleo has lots of places to go.

It's harder, in a way, to row slowly than it is to row quickly. But we have to keep it slow for the Doge, who doesn't want to arrive at his palace too soon, as he doesn't want it to be too obvious that he has nothing to do when he gets there. He is troubled: he longs for an immortality other than the generic one he will enjoy as an interchangeable Doge in Venetian civic paintings. He knows that no Doge is ever remembered by name by anyone except his mother. He resolves to be different. He will *do* something. "Forget it, Doge," I yell as I row. He sighs and reaches for another fig.

We have to stretch our trip on the Thames to accommodate the

"Water Music"—all of it. "Isn't this ever going to be over?" I gasp to the man in front of me, and he grunts in reply. The "Water Music" is a little repetitive, but the King likes it, and so we haul a whole orchestra up and down on the Thames several times a week.

Our canoe cuts silently through the water. I am the only woman at the oars. Nobody speaks. The leader of our party is scanning the North American coast for the smoke of campfires. When he sees some, we will go silently ashore and find out whose it is, friend or foe. After that, we will decide what to do.

Margaret, the physical trainer, stands before me. She wants me to row faster—ten strokes per minute faster. Easy for her to say: she probably has a negative body-fat index. My *ideas* weigh more than she does. But she is always nice to me, and she is proud of me for trying to row my 100,000 meters. I am not sure if I will really reach 100,000. But I will make myself stronger every time I row. I will help my heart. I feel muscles in my back and shoulders that women don't usually use.

We are all different. Some people are oppressed by a goal and despair when one is presented: *one more thing to fail at*. Others can't work unless they have one. I am both: I love a goal and a deadline, but I flirt with death through them, too, come too close to not meeting them, have to work too frantically as they approach.

If I make 100,000 meters, I'll get a T-shirt. If I don't, I won't. But either way, I'll have a great trip.

Believing the Bible

One of the reasons you can tell that Holy Scripture is inspired by God is by what happens when people read it together in Bible study groups. It causes them to listen to one another. The act of learning together opens the soul a little wider, every time.

When a priest is ordained, he or she must swear to a belief that the Scriptures are the word of God and contain everything necessary to salvation. The way in which we understand this vow sets us free: it doesn't have to mean that everything in Holy Writ is historically or journalistically true, but it does mean that everything there is the fruit of former generations' struggle to discern the will of God for them—the same struggle in which we also engage.

The Bible condemns sin. But sometimes it also enshrines it: certain passages in it assume the existence of slavery, for instance, and many others assume the inferior status of women. The ancient texts are holy, but holiness does not walk infallibly in this world. To enter into conversation with them from our place across the centuries is a holy enterprise, and no one should feel reluctant to engage them. The Bible contains what is necessary to salvation, including the invitation to enter into spirited and spirit-filled criticism of texts.

No one *should* feel reluctant to do this, but many people do. "Holy," for many of us, has always meant untouchable. The church would think it meant that, too, were it not for one thing: God was so willing to be touched that Jesus of Nazareth walked the earth, ate and drank, loved and laughed and cried. He touched us. He *came* to touch us. His holiness is not that of an idol in a temple. His is a holiness we can touch.

And we can touch those who have followed him in ages past.

Touch them and know them and argue with them. They were people like us. Inspired by God, as we can and *must* be today, if we are to follow a God who lives and not one who has died and left us a recipe book.

We honor the book, but we don't believe *in the book*.

We believe in God.

What Is God Doing?

The first reading for Morning Prayer is almost always a story. We just finished with poor old Job. We've wandered with the Israelites and watched them misbehave and get straightened out, marked the transfer of power to Joshua and heard about his wily ways of gaining military victory.

Now we're with Esther, the Jewish consort of a rather dim Persian king, named Ahasuerus (or maybe Xerxes, in your translation). Wicked Haman has persuaded the easily led Xerxes to embark upon a pogrom. We're currently in the thick of the drama: Haman and his awful wife have just had the happy thought of building a huge gallows on which to hang righteous Mordecai. Will they succeed?

I'm doing Esther this year. But next year I'll go with the alternate story: you can also read about Judith, who will seduce an Assyrian general, get him drunk, and cut off his head.

Of course, the readings for the Daily Office are intended to give us a fair-to-wide swath of Scripture through which to read in the course of a year. That's a most holy project, and should be commended. I am sure, though, that the morning ones are chosen for their luridness. We must leave our nice warm beds in the wee hours of the morning. We are barely awake when the Office begins. This will keep us coming back.

We need not watch Jerry Springer. We have incest, murder, intrigue, torture, lying, seduction, violence all within easy reach, lying right next to our beds on the nightstand, nestled within the covers of our Bibles.

The Old Testament is so violent, someone will say with a shudder. *Why do we have to read about these things?*

Yeah, it's pretty rough in spots. Those folks did a lot of begetting but also a whole lot of fighting. They identified their own military victories with the favor of God in a way we would not do today—or would we? I listen to the news and am not so sure.

We read them because they are the record of our forebears in faith, warts and all. We read them so we can come to our own conclusions about how God works in the world, having seen their conclusions. We read them and wonder what would do for us what the events of their lives did for them. We read about where they saw God. Where do we?

Something in your life shows God at work. The primary work of God on earth is bringing good out of evil. You miss the mark if you see evil and conclude that there is no God. Look straight at the evil, and then look right next to it: what is God bringing about? What can happen in the ashes of it?

In addition to the three-year cycle of Bible readings used for the Eucharist, there is a two-year cycle of readings known as the Daily Office, used for Morning and Evening Prayer. The story I refer to here is one of the Year Two, Proper 20 readings. If you want to know how to find and use the Daily Office readings, ask your parish priest to show you how to use the lectionary in the back of the prayer book (pp. 934–1001). He or she will be *thrilled* that someone wants to know.

Pictures of the Past

"I think it's the fact that the shutter had to stay open for such a long time that makes their eyes so penetrating," Q says. "They had to sit still for a long, long time because the shutter speed was so slow."

The eyes are remarkable. Light shines steadily from them in a way one does not observe in the efficient photographs of today. The eyes of nineteenth-century photographic subjects are deep pools of self-awareness and understanding. Even the children look wise. They look as if they already know what will happen.

PBS is airing Ken Burns's *The Civil War*, documenting the first war captured in photography. An immense collection of pictures from the early days of the photographer's art shows us every aspect of what that war was like for those who were there: battles and their aftermaths, wagon trains of artillery and infantry that go on for miles, hospitals, politicians, sudden cities of hundreds of white tents. The camera roams cemeteries, lingers over the dead faces of young soldiers, shows us a stiff hand raised in permanent supplication, stretches its gaze along a line of corpses that extends as far as it can see. It shows us women, at home and at the front, even children at the front, families left behind. We see the ruins of buildings, the wreckage of farms, lines of white crosses standing silent in fields of grass.

And a grainy motion picture from the early twentieth century: old, bearded men, marching together, being wheeled in chairs by younger men, leaning on canes. One of them shaves in a wash basin like the one he used when he was young. He is missing an arm. They are Civil War veterans, reenacting their living conditions at Gettysburg.

We see a president whose eyes grow sadder and sadder as the years grind on. It is almost as if his eyes tell us how he will die, before he knows it himself. The handsome, indecisive McClellan looks compassionately back at us: we can see that he is too shaken by the carnage of every encounter to take sufficient risks, and he hangs back from early encounters he could have won, making later, bloodier encounters inevitable. He does this repeatedly until he is removed. The flinty-eyed Grant manages just fine.

Nobody smiles for the camera. Nobody says "cheese."

Another war remarkable for its news coverage was the 1991 Gulf War. It bustled efficiently into our living rooms every night, its neat, triumphant "smart" bombs slipping smoothly down computer-simulated chimneys and exploding in neat expanding circles, its charts and graphs and electronic maps showing us how resoundingly and immediately we were winning.

There were no faces of the dead, though, in our living rooms. The war was sanitary, neat, ready for prime time, sexy even. Even the journalists were sexy, with their sleeveless khaki vests with lots of pockets that ordinary people—who were neither journalists nor soldiers—started wearing on the street. War was clean, surgical, and not very dangerous. And you could always change the channel.

The sad eyes of the Civil War subjects seem to look into our time. They seem to speak to us. They entreat us to remember, to heed. The eyes of modern subjects are caught in an instant, in less than an instant: they speak only of now. There is no time in our eyes. No time to learn, no time to regret, no time to warn anybody about anything. Just now. Just point and shoot.

Getting There

Sotheby's London is having an unusual auction. You can bid on Captain Bligh's compass. Or you can bid on the coconut shell from which he ate and drank after he was set adrift by the famous Bounty mutineers. It felt to them, I suppose, like a sentence of death to leave him and a few loyalists to face the Pacific in an open boat. But maybe not: they knew what a brilliant seafarer he was. He made Timor from the island of Tonga in about a month and a half, a distance of more than 3,600 miles.

I'm not doing badly myself. I rowed 6,000 meters yesterday, and took three minutes off my time, which I never would have done had not Margaret the trainer sat down at the rower next to me and said, "Come on, Barbara, let's move!" Then she took off at thirty-six strokes per minute, leaving me in the dust at twenty-three. I tried to get abreast of her at thirty-six; never got there, but I could hold it at thirty-one.

I would *never* have thought I could do that. Not in a million years. Last year at this time, I could barely walk up a flight of stairs.

We all have things we think we can't do. But what would it be like if we tried to do them anyway? One of two things would happen: we'd be able to do them, or we wouldn't. If we couldn't, we'd be in exactly the same place we are now. No loss. But if we could, we'd be someone a little different, defined a little more by a *can* than by a *can't*.

Little children are fountains of determined effort. They want to walk: first they pull themselves up on the edges of tables and circum-navigate them endlessly. Then they try to walk alone. It doesn't work. It doesn't work many, many times, but they don't stop doing it. They do not say to themselves, *Oh, well, I guess I'm just not a walker.* They try and try, try and fall, get up and try again.

And their limitless trying seems not to frustrate them, as failure frustrates us. They don't cry when they fall down in an attempt. They're too busy to cry, too intent on the task. They laboriously get up again and take another doomed step. And then one day they can do it.

Older people have an important function in the walking project: they are its cheerleaders. Parents and sisters and brothers are thrilled when babies take their first steps. They call each other up with the news, call the grandparents. They applaud wildly while the baby staggers around the living room. They record the moment in the baby book.

We need our obstacles. We need our failures. Nobody—well, Mozart, but almost nobody—sits down at the piano and tosses off a sonata the first time. The doting parents whose applause for "Chopsticks" and "Heart and Soul" quickly morphs into loathing need to get over the fact that God hasn't made their baby into Mozart. God already made Mozart.

And I will never be Margaret: older than I am, thin and muscled, in such superb condition that there appears to be nothing in the whole gym she can't do perfectly. But her high example and her shouts of encouragement have made me try harder, and I have gotten better.

So it works. And you never know until you try.

Why Bligh?

Bligh's coconut shell went for $111,135 at Sotheby's in London yesterday. That's a lot of money for an empty coconut. The bullet he used as a weight to measure out two ounces of bread a day went for $58,900. The article didn't say what they got for the compass he made by hand to use on the trip, or for his record of the voyage across the Pacific, but the whole lot fetched considerably more than a million dollars, so they must have done all right.

I guess somebody really *wanted to connect with the cantankerous old captain.*

I've got my mother's old metal measuring cup and her red-handled rolling pin. And her cool old cake pans with the piece that slides around the bottom of the pan to loosen the cake. And her favorite pie tin, which is my favorite, too.

Movers broke my grandmother's lovely gold-trimmed china urn, and I broke my other grandmother's lovely Swedish plate (and, in doing so, my own heart ... as if losing their dishes was the same as losing them). But Q glued all three of them back together, and you really can't tell.

In the twelfth and thirteenth centuries, romantic adventurers searched for the Holy Grail, the cup Jesus used at the last supper, or the cup that caught the blood that flowed from his side, or three or four other highly symbolic things a cup might do. Improbably, it was thought to be made of gold and studded with jewels, or carved out of a single large lapis lazuli. Where the penniless carpenter's son from Nazareth would have gotten such a thing remains a mystery. Not surprisingly, nobody's ever found the Grail.

If we have the cup he used, he will be closer to us.

But no. He is close to us already, as close in death as he ever was in life. And so are all the others. They are close to us, even closer, than they were in life. They are not bound as we are bound, isolated within our histories and our times, imprisoned within our bodies, confined to our own spaces. They are in Christ now—whoever they were, and wherever, and whenever—and Christ is as near to us as to all the ages, no more and no less.

Live and Let Live

Some plants can winter outside.

Some plants just die when it freezes.

And some plants come inside with us.

Some of the herbs are in pots in the kitchen window. Rosemary isn't in yet, but perhaps Q can bring her in by the end of the week. Basil hopes so—he's had a crush on her all summer. But Q's pretty busy this week: he's digging ivy out of the bed in front, and it's not going quietly.

The Christmas cactus has a new, wider pot and a new window. We'll see how he does. He outdid himself in his old window, blooming not only at Christmas, but on All Saints' Day as well. He is an Anglican, I guess. Or maybe a Druid.

The double-pink impatiens is going to become a houseplant this winter. A relative of hers did that last year with great success: bloomed inside all winter and then had a second summer's bloom outside on top of that. She's still blooming out there. I didn't know they had it in them.

I don't recall ever having seen a *Scilla siberica,* but we're going to have a cluster of them under the dogwood tree in the spring. Something strange is happening out there, by the way: all the crocuses are sending up leaves, as if it were early spring. I think the drought thoroughly confused them.

And the leaves are falling. It is said that the color will be short-lived this year, also an effect of the drought.

Soon it will be over. We'll turn the clocks back, and it will be dark every day by late afternoon. The plants will settle in for their naps. Some will just sigh quietly and die. The leaves will drift down over them, a blanket for the sleeping and the dead alike.

Those who have come inside will be flouting their natural rhythm.

They're supposed to die or go to sleep, but we make them stay up. Unlike people, plants don't think it's a treat to come inside. It's hard on them: not enough sun, not enough moisture in the air, too warm, no nighttime drop in temperature.

And you can tell by looking at them that it's hard. Their leaves grow thin and dull, and their stems weak. Sometimes their colors fade a bit. Aphids materialize out of nowhere, sensing the plants' weakness, and there are no natural predators in our living room to combat them.

Anthropomorphizing them as I do, I sometimes feel a little guilty about all our interference. I wonder if they would rather be dead than inside with us. I wonder if unnatural life is worse than no life at all. Sometimes I am not sure. Uncomfortably, I remember that bringing spring bulbs to winter bloom indoors is called "forcing."

Sometime in the next few weeks, Q will start bringing in his amaryllis farm. Perhaps it will be on a day I am in the city. The leaves of the amaryllis are about three feet tall—long, unattractive whips that have to be propped up with old skewers, sticks from outside, a toasting fork, or the plants will tip over under their own weight. They spend a couple of months down in the basement in the dark and then they come upstairs, enormous and green for months, until their fifteen minutes of fame arrive and they send forth lurid orange triple and quadruple blooms that look like something you'd see on *Star Trek*.

Live and let live. Or live and help to live. Or live and force to live. "Be fruitful and multiply," God told us, "and fill the earth and subdue it." We have certainly filled it. We dominate it. We bring it inside. We look at our plants and feel connected to the earth, create small artificial indoor springtimes in the midst of winter.

What we do with plants, we do with ourselves. We struggle to slow our aging, to extend our youth and beauty, extend life itself, sometimes, by artificial means. We're biased in favor of our own aggressive control over the forces of life. Family members of one who is mortally ill must be vigilant, insist on a gentle death sometimes, rather than a harshly maintained life that is not life at all. It is painful to choose death. But it is honest: we are not God. Spring and summer do not last forever. Life comes to an end. Sometimes it hurts to bow to that fact. Sometimes it hurts a lot. But it is better than forcing.

A Record of Your Life

What's your prayer routine like right now?
When do you pray, and where, and how?
What are you reading?
What's your current relationship with Scripture?
Do you journal?
Are you in recovery?
Have you ever made a confession?
Do you make retreats?

A person's first spiritual direction session includes a gentle inventory to see what spiritual practices are currently in place and how the directee thinks it's working, so that together we can begin to consider how it might become richer. There are probably a trillion different things a person can do to deepen his/her relationship with God, and nobody is going to do them all. But you have to start somewhere.

Sometime people wince when I take the inventory. They think their spiritual lives are not up to snuff. But the devotional life has nothing to do with snuff. And the fact that they have chosen to come for spiritual direction suggests that they have gotten the most important thing: there is always more for us.

If we knew how much God loves us, we would never be afraid we weren't doing it right. Never. God is doing it *so* right, we need not worry. All we have to do is show up and admit we don't know much.

The journal. The new directee looks regretful. "I'm not a very good writer," she begins apologetically. Oh good—then you'll be a fine journaler. You won't be trying to wow God with your brilliant turns of phrase.

Your journal should be free. Nobody need ever see it but you. It doesn't need full sentences or even complete ideas—it can be as literary or as un-literary as it wants to be. It can hold scraps of dreams that make no immediate sense, howls of indignation nobody else need ever see, rude questions to God about what on earth is going on. In fact, you aren't limited to just words. It can include *stuff*—stuff you find in the newspaper and clip, or a feather you find on your walk, or a leaf you pick up from the sidewalk, or a penny you saw in the gutter. It can hold tears. You can stain it with tears if you wish. You can draw in it.

Note the year somewhere near the front of your journal, and consider dating your entries. Someday, you're going to want to know when it was that you thought and felt the things you wrote in it. Later on, in the dry periods that come to all of us, going back through your journal may save your life. *I've been through this before and lived,* you'll say to yourself as you turn the old pages and read, *"Nothing.... Still nothing.... Where are you?... The weather is lovely and I couldn't care less.... Nothing.... I hate church.... Why am I such a hypocrite?..."* And you will not be able to deny better times, either; they'll be right there on the page: the time you pasted a leaf on a page and wrote a thank-you note for it; the time you understood something for the first time and wrote it down; the time you read an article and were suffused with irrational love for the complete stranger who was its subject, realizing that this must be something of what it is like to be God.

Cheap spiral notebooks or black and white composition books or elegant handmade blank books with arty covers—all are good. People accumulate quite a shelf of them once they acquire the habit. They read back through the years and laugh at themselves, give silent thanks for their very survival, catch their breath at God's goodness. They remember things long forgotten. They miss the dead. They see a long-ago flower, pressed flat. They retrace a familiar doodle in a margin. They close one of the oldest journals and feel almost wise.

Then they open a fresh one and smooth its blank pages. They pick up a pen and begin.

The Wall Between the Worlds

Helen wanted to go home. She lay in the hospital bed with her eyes closed and saw every beloved, comfortable thing: her potting room off the garage, plants everywhere; her kitchen with its generous workspace and a refrigerator papered with grandchildren's photographs; the trees in the garden outside the large windows, the birds at play in them. She saw their sitting area next to the kitchen, with its neat profusion of magazines, the couch by the phone, the pens. She saw her office, her desk, the hallway outside it, floor to ceiling with books and more photographs. Photographs of her children when they were little. Photographs of herself as a little girl, as a college girl, as a young woman, as a young mother, in middle age. Photographs with her husband, at home and in Maine, and at other homes from the past, in many places throughout the world. Photographs of her parents, her husband's parents, their long-gone aunts, cousins.

She saw her dining room, its generous table. She saw it empty, and she saw it filled with friends. She saw the art on the walls and the candles on the sideboard. She saw the photographs of animals on the walls as she made her way upstairs to their bedroom. She saw their bed, the pillows, their clothes in the closets, her shoes.

It was good to imagine home.

She dozed frequently, opening her eyes now and then to gaze at her children so as to save their faces to gaze upon again in dreams. She loved having them there with her, loved their faithfulness, loved their pulling together. She gazed at her husband, too, and loved it that he still came close to her, still kissed her, still touched her, even in such a place, at such a time, even when she was so weak. She saw a friend now and then, the rector of her church, her night nurse. There was the young rabbi from the hospital—there was something so right, somehow, about a lifelong Episcopalian praying with a rabbi at the end of her life. She smiled at the little joke of it.

For it *was* the end of her life. Still she could hope that it was not, but more and more it seemed to be. Her discomfort had ebbed away. She ate nothing, drank little. She could no longer hear well.

And yet, it was good.

People die as they live. The lives we have led surround us as we step out into our new lives. This is why it matters how we live, why it matters that we ponder the possibilities of the life beyond this life. It is a life about which we can know nothing. But we can know this life. We can explore its meaning. We can plumb it with every ounce of understanding we have. We can wonder about its spiritual depths, and we can listen quietly for the mysteries that connect it to larger mysteries. It will usher us to its edge, and then we will keep walking.

Helen sees now that the two lives are one. She is part of our world still, in a different way: closer to those she loves than it was ever possible to be when she lived here, one with God in a way that dissolves all the doubts and barriers she knew so well. And we are part of her world, too, although we don't know it yet. We join with her through the love we have always had with her. The body can die. Love can't. It is the only thing about us that endures.

So stay tuned. The wall between the worlds is very thin in spots.

Lady Poverty

A select cadre of eMo readers is already awake and at work when the eMo goes out, which is usually at about 5:30 or 6:00 in the morning. Sometimes earlier, sometimes later, if I oversleep. Others find it in their email a few hours later, when they settle at their desks to begin the day's correspondence. Some don't get to their computers until nighttime. And, for some, it's not early morning now: they live in other parts of the world, and soon it will be tomorrow.

Monastics have been up for a long time. As I write, I listen to recordings of their chant. I even look at ancient pictures of them, sometimes: sitting straight on their hard benches in their chapels on cold mornings, their hands under their scapulars: it is the proper place for their hands, but it also keeps them warm. I think of them, in ages past and today: their discomforts and deprivations, their ongoing firm duty of prayer, their earnest desire that it become more than duty, that prayer become words of love for them.

Even today, it is a hard life. Not to own things oneself, in our culture, is a radical thing. We view adulthood as a process of increasing autonomy: it is hard to set that aside and place it under the discernment of a group.

"Lady Poverty," St. Francis called it, with a typical courtliness, and served her radically. Poverty of possessions, to be sure, but also poverty of power, poverty of spirit, that sacred sense of waiting emptiness, waiting to be filled by God alone.

Here is the risk: if I give everything away, will God supply what I need? If I go out on a limb, will God be there? You don't have to be a nun or a monk to ask that question. We're all asking that question every time we're faced with something scary that forces our reliance on God.

Like turning down money.

Like confronting someone you love about behavior that is unworthy of him.

Like saying no to something you want for the wrong reasons.

Like letting go of a love that degrades instead of ennobles.

Like accepting physical weakness.

Like letting someone you love make his own mistakes.

Will God really be with me if I do this, if I surrender the power I think I have?

The monks blow surreptitiously on their fingers to warm them so they can turn the pages of their breviaries. The nuns can see the clouds of their own breath. The Office comes to its end, and everyone files out of the chapel to the refectory. The monastics of the thirteenth century have water and bread for breakfast. The modern ones get coffee and granola.

Some things are much easier now.

And some things are much harder.

A Question of Cannas

"We can just knock on the door if they're home. It looks like their lights are on."

The odds were good: it was suppertime. It was their canna lilies that caused us to invade: a lovely stand of remarkable, tall plants, blooms still coming out on top, even in mid-October. Ours are still blooming, too. As tenders of similarly talented canna lilies, we had a question.

"Hello, my name is Barbara Crafton, and this is my husband, Richard Quaintance. We love your garden. Do you have a moment to answer a question about your canna lilies?"

No gardener ever minds that kind of question. They never mind a little gentle showing off. This one had some off to show, all right: the cannas were lovely, of course, but a remarkable angel's trumpet plant out front still sported Easter-lily-size blooms on a strange long stem. She told us we could go out back and take a look, too, if we wanted. Out back, she assured us, was *really* special.

Out back we went, while they returned to their chilling supper. But it was only a moment before they were out the back door to join us, unable to resist our delight in their garden. And delight it was: they have a little pool! With wonderful rocks! And a waterfall! And nice, fat fish swimming in it! And wonderful plants, some of which we don't have! I began to feel a little faint.

The woman is a ceramicist, and her interesting work rests here and there in the garden. It is a tiny little space, not a third the size of ours, but everything in it is loved and lovely. At the end of the garden, I glimpsed a small pair of images: St. Francis and St. Clare. Nice to know we have mutual friends.

Autumn is the time when growing stops and goes underground.

Freed of our more intense schedules relating to keeping track of the burgeoning summer, we retreat to our dreams of the future: plants we will procure; where we will put them; what we will move where; whether we can have a pond with a waterfall, and where.

Dreams, also, of what will happen without our input. Some things will multiply down there in the dark, sending up three daffodils where there were only two last year. The echinacea I planted along the side may do something interesting next year, luring bees and butterflies over to that side of the house. The hollyhocks may or may not make it through the winter: it all depends on how deeply they establish themselves in the little time they have left.

There is something relaxing about having done all you can, even if you don't know whether your efforts will be crowned with success. It's no longer up to me, what happens with the hollyhocks. Every bloom is a gift, composed only partly of anything I may or may not have done.

In the end, all you can do is all you can do. Once you have done that, your role is done. And you wait in peace for what comes next.

How Happy Do You Want to Be?

The people who put the lectionary together weren't stupid. They made sure, all those years ago, that right about now we would be hearing readings from Scripture—and then homilies—about money, just when churches are getting ready to ask for some. The Sermon on the Amount, as they say.

"What's your honorarium?" a church will ask me when we're talking about my coming to speak or teach. I tell them what my daily fee is, and then I tell them that I expect rich churches to pay that much and poor churches to pay what they can, and that I leave it up to them to decide whether they are a rich church or a poor church. I'm really no help at all.

"Is it lawful to pay taxes to Caesar, or no?" they asked Jesus. Give us a rule, something that will always be right, something we can just put into place and then never think about again. Deliver us, please, from having to exercise our judgment.

But requests for a rule always generate more questions than they solve. "Whose likeness is this?" Jesus asks, showing his questioners a coin. Three guesses. "Then render to Caesar the things that are Caesar's, and to God the things that are God's."

Oh.

But wait a minute: that's no help. *Everything* is God's. That which a coin symbolizes is wealth—gold, perhaps, the wealth in terms of the goods it will buy. The wealth of the earth—mineral, animal, vegetable, whatever. It's all God's. Caesar's in charge of a lot of it at the moment, but this is all God's stuff. We're subletting.

How much shall I give?

Give to God what is God's.

But that's everything.

I know.

How much should I give?

Depends. Are you rich or poor?

How much should I give?

Depends. How blessed are you?

How much should I give?

Depends. How eager are you to see things happen?

How much should I give?

Depends. How happy do you want to be?

Because that's the odd thing about giving back to God the gifts God first gave to us: it makes us happy. Unexpectedly so, in comparison with the feeling we get paying other bills. I suppose that's because giving it back puts us in the right place in relation to our money, and our rapacious culture so wants us to be in the wrong place: anxious, unsatisfied, so that we will buy things to try to assuage our pain.

The moment you give money to something that will heal, you're reminded of your health. The moment you give to the poor, you're reminded of your great good fortune in having a roof and a meal. When you give to provide a place for community to grow and flourish, you remember immediately how blessed you have been in it, and how important it is for you that it continue to be a blessing in the world.

This piece was written in anticipation of the Gospel reading for Proper 24, Year A: Matthew 22:15–22.

We're All on the List

I did not survive the rowing challenge at the gym.

Well, I *survived*. I'm alive. But I did not make it to 100,000 meters in the allotted month. I came in at 62,000 and change.

Yesterday I climbed the stairs and saw the bulletin board, where they put healthy messages about cholesterol and vegetables for us to ponder as we begin our workouts. There was a computer printout of all the names of the people who entered the rowing challenge. A tiny stab of envy: I knew my name wouldn't be there. I hadn't made the grade. I hadn't passed.

The challenge embraced many gyms, not just ours at the Y. There were hundreds of names on the sheets of computer paper. The names of people from our Y were highlighted yellow. I scanned them dispiritedly— *and there was my name.*

They put me on the list anyway.

How nice, I thought. *How kind.* The top guy from our gym rowed something like 420,000 or 510,000 meters. That's many times across the lake. I didn't come close to him.

But I was on the list. I was in the race. I did what I did. They didn't just recognize the stars. They recognized all of us. I wasn't going to be a star this time. I was just part of us. And we were on the list.

And I discovered that I love rowing. Love the feeling of using my back and shoulder muscles. Love the fact that they got stronger during the month of rowing, that I can bench press ten more pounds now than I could when it started, and lift ten more in the preacher curl, as well. Love the fact that I can do any of this stuff at all. At this time last year I was becoming very ill, dangerously so. Weak and exhausted and full of pain. And now I am better.

The challenge is over, so I don't have to sit down at the rower if I don't want to. I can use any piece of equipment in the gym. I decide I'll spend most of my time on the treadmill, but first I visit my old friend. I sit down and put my feet in the stirrups, set the resistance dial to the highest number I've ever used just to see how it goes, and begin. I row 2,500 meters, just for old time's sake.

Hey, it says, *good to see you back. I wasn't sure you'd come and visit after the challenge was over.*

I look around the gym. During the rowing challenge, there were often peeved-looking men waiting for the two rowing machines, looking pointedly at their watches, sighing heavily. Nobody.

I didn't finish the challenge, I tell it as we cut through imaginary water.

Aw, hell, that don't matter, it says, moving so fast that our wake splashes a little water into the boat.

How about that guy who rowed 410,000? I said.

That meatball? the machine says. *Look, don't worry about him. Don't worry about nobody else. Just come and see me sometimes, okay? You're gonna have the strongest back and shoulders you ever dreamed of. You're gonna forget what a backache is, babe.*

Did you just call me "babe"?

Sorry. I don't remember your name. Never forget a face, ya know?

I'm Barbara. Barbara Crafton.

Oh, yeah. 62,000 and change. Nice goin'.

Thanks.

A Hidden God

Few things in life are as irrevocable as having pressed "send." The damage is done when you have pressed "send." You're not going to be able to beg the post office guy to give you your letter back on this one. Nobody's going to be able to kick you under the table as a signal that you should shut up now. It is an action the consequences of which are stern, immediate, and utterly final.

I just did it. You'll see, if you haven't already: I sent a blank message to everyone on the eMo list, and that's a lot of people. *Damn,* I said silently as the eNothing shot out into the ether, never to return.

Q looked grave when I came home last night. "I want to talk to you about your spelling," he said.

What a great idea, I said to myself. It had been a long day. I knew he was talking about a typo in a recent eMo, but which one? The one in which I typed "they" for "there?" "No" for "not?" "Ever" for "never?"

It was "ever" for "never." "It changes the meaning of the sentence," he said.

No kidding, I said silently.

"Can't you read things over before you send them?" he asked.

We will leave the record of the conversation at this point, I think. It's very early in the morning.

Actually, I do read these things over before I send them. I usually read them twice. I use spell-check, for what that's worth. I just don't pick up everything. I usually don't pick up at least one thing in each eMo. No, I take that back: I almost *always* pick it up. Just after I have pressed "send."

Damn.

He wants me to let him proofread before I send things out. Maybe

I should. He is one of the world's champion copy editors, a proofreader of the gods. I should let him go over them before they go out.

At five in the morning? Wake him up to proofread? We'd be on *Judge Judy* in no time.

But couldn't I wait? Couldn't I wait until a little later and send the eMo then, brand-spanking-proofread and ready to go?

To my natural impatience, burnished to a brilliant sheen over many bullheaded years, I add the desire that those who get the eMos—in this hemisphere, anyway—have them first thing, that they will be there in the inbox as a kind of prayer. I pray before I write them. They are a continuation of morning devotion for me. However far afield they may range—snakes, pies, geraniums, the cat What's-Her-Name (and What's-Her-Name is *very* far afield)—they are always about God. They are intended to reveal God's hand, "hid from our eyes," as it says in a beautiful old hymn.

God is often hidden. But God is not hiding. We can look carefully, with sharp eyes, sharp minds, sharp spirits, and we can see where God is.

And right next to where God is, something will be misspelled or misplaced. Don't just look among the perfect for the hand of God, and don't just look with your own perfections. Look among the errors, and look with your own mistakes.

A Most Excellent eMo

It helps if I have an idea of what the morning's eMo will be about when I go to bed the night before. Just one idea is enough—I don't need to write the thing in my mind before I type it out on the computer. I just need a thought.

I had a great one last night. I was a little surprised that I hadn't thought of writing it before, it was such a good idea. It was so good that I wondered if I shouldn't reserve it for a more extended essay in my book on middle age, instead. *This is going to be excellent,* I thought happily as I drifted off, *One of the truly great eMos*.

In the morning it was gone. I woke up, tickled pink about my great idea, ready to get up and begin—and discovered it was no longer there. *Maybe after I've done Morning Prayer,* I thought, and turned on the computer to boot up while I prayed. Maybe the sound of the machine would remind me what I was going to write, sort of like Pavlov's dogs, which became conditioned to salivate when they heard the dinner bell. Nothing.

Damn. It was such a good one.

Names of people I know really well. Things on mental grocery lists. What I did last night. What I'm supposed to do today. What I was going to say. Lines of dialogue I thought I'd never forget from plays in which I was completely immersed for weeks on end. The Apostles' Creed. Good Lord!

Strange when memory begins to fail like that. To grope for words, to reach for an idea and find myself snatching at the air, the idea's ghost disappearing in an amorphous vapor just above my head. I have several friends who are terrified of Alzheimer's Disease: every forgotten name, every obliterated engagement feels to them like the beginning of the end. Perhaps, for some of us, it *is*.

Losing the capabilities on which we have always relied will change our futures. But we will still *have* a future, a life to be lived until it is ended by death. There will still be people who love us, people charged with making sure we're safe. We will have unexpected moments of enjoyment, tiny satisfactions—very small ones, then, not like now, but not nothing, either. Even the profoundly ill are still people, still worthy of care, still beloved of God.

All of us are only temporarily able-bodied and of sound mind. We don't know when that will change. For almost all of us, it will be before we're ready—we will never be ready. The healthy often tell me they fear becoming ill or weak, and sometimes inform me that their lives will not be worth living if they lose their ability to walk, to see, to think. That if these things should happen, they just want to die.

And there are moments when death is no longer the enemy. For all of us, it will one day be a welcome relief from suffering and exhaustion. In my experience, though, those moments come to most people long after the healthy think that they will. Even profoundly limited life is still life, and treasured beyond what those of us blessed with a high standard of living might think.

A Mercy Killing

"We're going to be late if we don't get going," I told Rosie. But neither of us moved. We were riveted to the television screen, watching a baby rhinoceros being born. His enormous mother paced uncomfortably around her stall, walking backwards in a vain attempt to equalize the enormous pressure of the baby pushing against her to get out. Then, with an impossible stretching of skin, the baby rhino tumbled out onto the bed of clean straw awaiting its arrival. We both cheered softly.

"Their pregnancies take fourteen months," Rosie informed me as we walked to the car.

Wow. I thought nine was bad.

We wouldn't be late. We made good time on the Parkway, and soon we were cruising along Broad Street in Red Bank, trying to find my doctor's office along the avenue of Victorian mansions.

Suddenly, ahead in the road, something terrible to see: a squirrel had just been hit by a car. His nether half was flattened to a bloody smear on the asphalt. Incredibly though, his top half was still alive. He pitched and flailed frantically in a doomed struggle to flee his agony, but could not rise—he had no legs left.

"Oh!" I cried. I knew what I must do. I aimed right for him.

"No, Mamo!"

I did it: I hit him squarely. We both felt the tire go over his little body.

"Sweetie, I'm so sorry."

She was too shocked to say anything. Her eyes were wide.

"I had to end it for him. Do you understand?"

Silence. I thought she might cry, but she did not.

"I'm sorry, Honey."

Her eyes were still wide, and she was still silent.

"He couldn't get away, and he would have had to suffer there. I had to end it quickly."

She nodded.

"I'm so sorry."

That night, I told Q. "*That'll* be an eMo," he said.

"I don't know—you think the eMo community will embrace a squirrel killer?"

A mercy killing, the doctor had called it when we arrived at her office, shaken.

A mercy killing.

I, who am not God, who have no authority over life and death, took a life into my hands and ended it because I thought it was best. It was a tiny life, and it was coming to a terrible end, but the act was enormous.

On the television, the mother rhinoceros was aided by her human companions in a difficult birth. Perhaps she would have died without their intervention. The squirrel was different. We no longer had a choice between life and death for the squirrel. It was not so lucky. The only choice was between protracted agony and quick release. I'd do it again.

But I'll never forget it.

Stocking up on Martha

"How many should I get, do you think?" I asked Anna.

"Oh, gosh—get as many as you can," she replied.

Variety Village here in town, the store where you can find anything, sometimes has a load of books for little or nothing. I've gotten current bestsellers there for $3 or $4. I got a wonderful gardening book there for $5 just a few weeks ago. And now, pay dirt: Martha Stewart's 2002 book, all the recipes that appeared in her magazine throughout 2001 and—as if that weren't bounty enough—her *Desserts* book. For $5 each. I gasped when I saw them, dozens of them, in perfect condition, one with a perfect six-layer Italian Cream Cake on a creamy white plate on the cover and the other with a picture of perfect Martha herself, blonde and smiling, one hand raised in an airy oh-it's-nothing-really gesture as she nibbled a bit of meringue from a tart she was placing in an antique pie rack. I snatched up three of each and took them home.

I like her even better now that it appears she's an insider trader. This is odd—insider traders hurt people with their peculiar form of stealing, and that's not nice. But I can't help it.

"Maybe you should go back and get some more," Anna said. "We could use them for Christmas presents. I mean, those are $35 books."

She was right. I couldn't afford *not* to get them. I was *making* money buying them. I went back and got two more of each, making six total.

Except this time they were $4, not $5. Wow. Martha's stock really *is* going down.

"You've always reminded me of her," I wrote in the copy I used as a bread-and-butter gift when we went to the home of friends for dinner last night. The hostess opened it to the inscription and hooted with laughter.

I have read that Martha, when her daughter was born, planted an avenue of trees for the girl to walk down when the time came for her to get married. I believe this. I can just see her, struggling out of the stirrups and off the delivery table, hobbling out to the front of the house in her hospital nightie, grabbing a spade on the way out.

When the girl did grow up and get married, though, she did it in City Hall. In a grey pants suit. She more or less *had* to, if you ask me.

That must have just about killed Martha. But she handled it well, even wrote graciously about it in her magazine. ImClone is not Martha's first disappointing experience.

They say that the whole Martha, Inc. empire is in danger, because she sells herself as a brand and the brand is compromised by the financial scandal. I wonder. I think, rather, that in the Martha, Inc. scandal we are about to witness the audience's willing suspension of disbelief on a scale hitherto unimagined. She is so important as a household goddess that her admirers will probably allow her to be crooked, ethically flawed, like the Greek gods and goddesses, with their shabby intrigues and petty jealousies. It is esthetic perfection people buy from Martha, not moral rectitude. As long as her cakes continue to rise, she'll always have a home.

Or six.

Handmade

The India Room is coming along nicely. Its color scheme is as follows: pale fuchsia walls, red bedspread with a gold vine print on it, an old rug in cream with flowers in different colors; another old Turkish rug of tan and blue on black; a shell lamp of colored glass, mainly red; a telephone completely covered with animal and flower stickers in colors too numerous to mention; a wicker armoire and table trimmed in blue and coral; a wicker chair with a purple-flowered seat cushion; a purple wandering Jew plant by the window and bouquets of dried roses on top of the armoire in all colors into which God allows roses to fade.

All it really needs now are panel curtains in several shades of gold, olive green, purple and red, and I think the window blinds need to be painted with acrylics in rough stripes of colors I haven't made up my mind about yet. They're white now—ugh. I just don't understand some people's color choices.

But the loveliest thing in the India Room is the cover on top of the bedspread. It is very old, and traveled back with us in my suitcase from Tamil Nadu. It is green and black, with orange and black embroidery, strewn with tiny mirrors and pearls, each sewn on separately. There is a patch in the middle of it, where it was worn out by somebody sleeping under it: the patch isn't quite the same shade, nor was it applied by the same hand. The stitches are different, and there are no pearls there. *Life goes on*, it says. *Do the best you can with what you have.*

I go to the India Room when my leg hurts at night, because its mattress is more comfortable than ours. And because I like the way it looks. And the way it smells: it smells of sandalwood and old roses, of lavender and incense. And today, it also smells of ...What's-Her-Name.

I have raised two children and diapered dozens more besides.

Mine had digestive tracts like everyone else's, and I am not squeamish. But cats are a different species. Peeing on things is a major form of communication among them, second only to mewing and howling. They think they can claim a space by baptizing it. And they're right— I'm certainly not sleeping in there again until I've gotten rid of What's-Her-Name's unmistakable mark.

She got the antique throw. Hoping against hope that she might have shown some respect for age and domestic art, I buried my nose in it. That was a mistake.

Q has spoken to the vet about this. The vet says we can bring What's-Her-Name in for counseling. $55 an hour for that cat to lie on a couch and talk about her childhood? We're just not sure how we feel about that, especially since the vet says What's-Her-Name really doesn't even have to *come* to the counseling, that we can just come ourselves. There's something fishy about the whole thing, if you ask me. Makes you wonder for whom this counseling is really intended.

Besides, I have a more immediate problem on my mind: what to do about the antique bedcover. I can't trust all those pearls and mirrors to a dry cleaner. It can't go in a washing machine. I must do what they would do in India, where it was made: take it outside to the riverbank and run water repeatedly through it until it is clean, working over each area of it with a stone. Then let it dry flat on a rock.

The nearest river is the Hudson, which is now cleaner than the Ganges but still not what I want next to my skin. And we don't have broad rocks to lay things on in Metuchen. I will use the garden hose and let it lie on the grass until it is dry.

Maybe I should hang it on the wall instead of spreading it on the bed. Maybe I should hang it from the canopy frame on top of the bed in there, so that the only people who saw it were the people sleeping in the bed—they would awaken to a sky of mirrors and pearls. That might be nice. We shall see.

The people who used it first are dead. The people who made it are dead—they probably didn't live long lives, and the lives they lived were hard. Cross-legged for hours and hours on the dirt floor of their house, inside in dim light, away from the blinding heat of the South Indian sun, they worked away, held pearls in place and affixed them with tiny stitches, slipped the little mirror into pockets of folded fabric and stitched them down securely, pieced together green and black cloth. Maybe the whole family worked on it, staking a whole season's food on its satisfactory and timely completion.

I have always thought it striking that modern design is so simple, when mechanization would make it possible to make complicated things quickly. We don't, though: our vases are simple swoops of polished glass or gleaming plastic. Our chairs are blocky and severe, or curves of steel like a fall of water. We have no ball-and-claw feet, no cabriole legs, no turned finials. We could make all those things quickly with our machines, and in reproductions of *old* furniture we certainly do, but in the best of modern design, we don't. Modern design speaks of machine. It does not speak of hand.

Who is to say which is better? The family sitting on the floor in the heat of midday, stitching frantically to secure its own meager living? Or the factory worker, pouring white-hot steel into a mold from which a chair emerges whole? The finished tapestry of pearls and mirrors and thousands of stitches? Or the simple swath of uniform color and texture?

All I can say is this: when it was very hard to do so, people sat cross-legged on the floor and created beauty. And it survives them, whispering their names.

Why Me?

"Mamo!" Rosie said, shocked. "Are you all right?"

"Hold onto the rail, girls!" I said from the bottom of the back stairs, down which I had disappeared abruptly from their view. We had new back stairs put in this summer, and their finish is a lovely one, worthy of a piece of furniture. It has just occurred to me that something offering a little more traction might have been a better choice. But I'm not sure it would have made any difference in this weather: freezing rain, our first of the season, and everything outside was acquiring a coat of ice.

I hauled myself up and surveyed the damage. Both knees and my right hand, injured in the vain attempt to break my own fall: instinctive, but it never works. I would live.

As the girls crept carefully down the glittering stairs and into the car, I sat at the wheel and brooded over the fall. Not over the injuries—I'm only now feeling them this morning. Not over the fear of falling, something I have fought since I broke my back years ago. I brooded over something else: a sense of shame that washes absurdly over me when I get hurt. I am flooded with shame when something bad happens to me. Always.

How weird.

Why? Why should a person feel ashamed of falling down? But I do. I scold myself. *Stupid! Clumsy! You get right up this minute and stop being such a baby!* a harsh voice within says, and, meekly, I obey.

The Hebrew Scriptures usually assume that physical ills and mishaps are the result of sin. In Psalm 41:4, "I said, 'Lord, be merciful to me; heal me, for I have sinned against you.'" In the books of the Kings, sin is confidently assigned to just about everyone who dies—"So he died, because of the sins he had committed, doing evil in the eyes of

---

the Lord," as if they'd all have lived forever, if only they had behaved themselves.

But even in the Hebrew Scriptures, there are voices of those who know otherwise. In the Book of Job, where "shit happens" is encountered in its most ancient surviving form of that basic wisdom. In the fatalistic verses of Ecclesiastes. And this more careful analysis of human sorrow continues in the words of Jesus, who refuses to play with those people who ask, "Who sinned, this man or his parents, that he was born blind?"

We feel less vulnerable if we can believe we make our own destiny. "Well, if I can just do all the right things, I'll escape trouble," we think hopefully. We'd rather accept blame for suffering we did not author than admit the truth—that it just happens to us sometimes. For no reason. With no plan. That my behavior didn't cause it and my behavior isn't going to make it go away. That it's out of my hands.

This morning I can hardly type, and the knee with the heartiest love of complaint really has something to gripe about. *Damn,* I think. *What did I do to deserve this?*

Nothing. Fell down a slippery set of stairs. That's all.

Eye of the Beholder

Computer problems again. I had been trying various schemes to send out my latest eMo successfully, but nothing worked. I checked again at 5:30 A.M. Nope. Still nothing. But I *did* discover several lovely emails from my Geranium Farm friends and several much less lovely emails from perfect strangers: three invitations to buy bedsheets, a suggestion that I might want to go to Monaco or St. Kitts, and something about enlarging my penis—when I get one.

We all remember when Spam was just a brand of potted meat. Those days are gone, as gone as the days when Madonna was just the Blessed Mother of Our Lord Jesus Christ. The use of the term for junk email is appropriate, though: the old Spam was made of a variety of unwanted cow innards and scraps of pigs' feet, thrown together in enormous pots to cook and then pressed into countless rectangular cans to be fed, initially to soldiers as cheap rations in World War II and eventually to the rest of us. I've always been somewhat surprised that the old Spam did as well as it did, but I am utterly astonished by the proliferation of the new spam. Somebody must be biting; otherwise every man, woman, and child in American wouldn't be greeted each and every morning by the same two Viagra ads.

Some eMo recipients' email programs think the eMos are spam because they come from a large list. I receive plaintive messages from people who long for eMos they can call their very own, yet can't seem to receive them, and we have to work together to get their machines to recognize me as a friend. Usually replying to an eMo accomplishes that—the machine must feel that, if we have exchanged notes even once, we must know and like each other. For whatever reason, it calms down and lets the eMos pass.

Once in a while, it is the recipient who thinks my eMos are spam. "This is very annoying," a man wrote to me yesterday. "Take my name off this list." I always respond sweetly to such rejection, hoping to make the sender feel guilty. "I'm sorry the eMos have been a burden," I type back. "You're off the list." *Philistine,* I add silently, but I don't type that.

I guess spam is in the eye of the beholder.

One just never knows. Twenty-three years of preaching have taught me that the sermon I thought was dead on arrival will turn out to have been just what someone in the congregation needed to hear. Go figure. And the one I thought was especially witty and wise evokes the dread words, "Thank you for your message," at the door, an infallible sign that they didn't hear a word. You just don't know.

You usually can find what you need on the Internet.

You may see God in an eMo.

 If we are looking for God, we are likely to find God. Because God is always seeking us, and waits for us in ordinary places.

No Grownups Allowed

The people in the large, expensively-restored Victorian at the end of Rector Street go all-out in all their external decorations for the holidays. Now, they have strings of tiny orange lights hanging from their trees, jovial goblin faces on the front doors where they put the Christmas wreaths, little white ghosts in the fetching window boxes.

I don't remember Halloween decorations on this scale when I was a girl. It wasn't nearly as ornate a holiday—you just threw a sheet over your head, and out you went, begging candy from the neighbors. As elaborate as anybody ever got was to carve a pumpkin and set it out on the porch (whereupon kids from the neighborhood would make off with it and smash it on the road). In school, we took colored construction paper and cut out black cats with arched backs and pumpkins with triangle noses and eyes and toothy grins or scowls, and put them in the windows. That was it.

Q came home with some gourmet cookies from the supermarket. "We can give these out on Halloween." But uh-oh: they're not individually wrapped. Vigilant baby-boomer parents will never permit their darlings to accept them, not from disheveled old people who live in a purple house. Kids probably tell each other stories about us already. Just let us try giving them unwrapped cookies.

We'll just have to eat them ourselves.

The lives of children have changed in recent years. Little is as I remember. They can't play outside unattended—I don't remember the term "play date" from my youth, or from my children's childhoods. They can't wander through the Internet—the twelve-year-old pen pal they meet online might be a forty-nine-year-old child molester. They can't go to the store by themselves, or walk to school. I look back at the hours and hours of unmonitored time I had as a child. It can't happen today.

But not everything has changed. I walk to the train, and pass a neighbor's house. There, at the foot of one of their trees, the little girl next door has built a miniature world: acorns all in a circle, a tiny house built of twigs, a little fence of more twigs. A place for an imaginary small friend. I made just such a place when I was little, telling myself that it would always, always be there, that a hundred years from then I would return and find it intact.

I itch to add to her small world, to leave a calling card, some sign that another girl saw it and realized what it was. But I pass it by. It is not for me. I am not another girl, now. I am not in this game.

Heavenly Geographic

When I was a chaplain on the waterfront, we used to store magazines in a rusty old shipping container—the long box you see on an eighteen-wheeler. It was packed to the ceiling with them: *Sports Illustrated*, *Scientific American*, *Smithsonian*, *Popular Mechanics*. Those were popular on the waterfront, for that overwhelmingly male population. Cooking magazines fared better than one might think, too: the cooks wanted them. But no women's magazines and no porn (I imagine many would have appreciated the latter, but it would have been unseemly for chaplains—especially *lady* chaplains—to arrive bearing skin magazines). *Field and Stream* did well. *Audubon.* Anything in Spanish went like hotcakes.

But the hands-down winner among seafarers was *National Geographic.* They are prized on board, passed around eagerly—you can be but a halting speaker of English and still enjoy *National Geo.* Many times I would bring one on board and be shown an article about the home of the man standing right before me, pictures of sights he knew well, pictures of life in the city of his birth.

The container got too full too quickly. One of us would have to get out there and clean it out, making order out of the chaos of magazines in stacks as tall as we were.

It was dangerous. I kept getting hijacked by *National Geographic*, stopping to look at pictures of great beauty, at faces of people who lived far from Port Newark, at lives lived differently from the way I lived my life. At the little African boy standing in front of his hut, sadly cradling his dead goat in his arms. At Koko the gorilla, tenderly cuddling her little golden kitten. At the exquisitely beautiful Afghan girl, looking steadily at us with her amazing green eyes. At Winston Churchill, staring fiercely from the cover of the issue that reported on his 1964 funeral. I remember receiving that issue in 1964—it contained a little phonograph record you could play to hear part of the funeral.

Once I was hijacked by an issue devoted to photographs taken by the Hubble telescope. Hubble has been out there for ten years now. After a panicky moment in which it appeared that the thing wasn't going to work, that the millions and millions of dollars and years and years of work it represented were going to hurtle endlessly through space without sending us even one image—the NASA engineers interviewed during those days all but wept on television—Hubble began to transmit, and has done so steadily ever since.

And what pictures! Supernovae and planets, nebulae, Saturn with its rings, the moons of Jupiter, a galaxy shaped like a tadpole and called by that name, another shaped like a whirlpool and called by *that* name. Planets and stars surrounded by hot gases that refract the light, so that we see them as red, as purple, as orange, as rainbows and golden spangles. Beauty at which one could stare for hours.

The container was not heated. I would lean against the wall and look at pictures until my fingers ached and I had to give up and get busy, get the blood circulating again. Then I would make up a few packs and head out to the ships, plop the magazines down on a table in the messroom, where the seafarers would set on them like locusts. "Now, you share!" I would admonish, shaking my finger like a teacher, and they would nod and laugh.

The seas upon which they sail are still only slightly less mysterious than the heavens in which the rings of Saturn and the Whirlpool Galaxy ride. The seas, too, are dangerous—seafaring is safer now than it has ever been in the history of navigation, and still a ship goes down somewhere in the world every three days. They leave their homes and do not know if they will return, as Hubble left its launching pad and seemed, for a time, to disappear into the nothingness of space. They understand their own smallness, seafarers, and the vastness of the sea upon which they sail.

To read about places far away. Places not even on this earth. Places we will never see. To have them brought close to us. Other places and other times—the tomb of Tutankhamen, the bog men, the mummified sacrificial victims of vanished Peruvian religious rites—to read about them and see them is to understand our smallness. There is much that I do not know. And the hidden sides of things I do know—the lives of birds and insects, the mysteries of life under the sea, the unseen forces of molecules. I see, as I turn the pages, that I know almost nothing.

How lovely to think that I can see these things by the work and wit of others. That curiosity—longing to know for the sake of knowing—is part of what it is to be a human being. That we gather and cooperate for this purpose, reach across lines of national enmity and suspicion because we want to see, want to know.

The Holy Spirit is identified with Wisdom. With Wisdom, but also with the breath of life. It's not just an option with us, to wonder and learn, not just something that some people do. It is part of the very stuff of life, part of what keeps us alive. At the end of life, when we can no longer speak, those who love us will wonder if we know: *Do you think she knows me? Can she hear me? Does she know what's happening?* And, when knowing is over, the earthly good-bye is final. And another knowing begins.

All Saints'

It was the Sunday of the New York Marathon—when anything can happen, traffic-wise—and so I left early in order to reach St. Paul's in Brooklyn on time. But there was nothing untoward on the roadways. I sailed through the Holland Tunnel, selected because I knew the Verrazano would be a sea of runners, zipped down the West Side Highway. The hollow feeling in my stomach that passing the World Trade Center site always gives me was still there, but I cruised on past and into the Brooklyn Battery Tunnel, emerging among the low buildings and sunny streets of Brooklyn. I parked right in front of the church. It was just nine o'clock. Mass was at eleven. Plenty of time.

I went to buy the paper. The streets with old Brooklyn names— Sackett, Woodhull, Degraw—were quiet: a few dog walkers, other people sauntering home with the *Times* under one arm, a few parents with toddlers in the park. The venerable brownstones were still decorated for Halloween: the children of Carroll Gardens clearly enjoy that holiday, and witches and pumpkins lingered, unmolested, on the stoops.

Soon the church was open. I heard them before I saw them: the organ, the choir rehearsing for the coming service, the quiet deliberate footsteps of the clergy and quicker ones of acolytes preparing the sanctuary. Two men made their way along the front of a side chapel with a ladder, lighting candles high above the ground for this observation of All Saints'.

Richard Upjohn designed this church: it is airy and spacious, light pouring through as many Gothic windows as he could include in its walls. Its gleaming wooden floor imparts warmth that stone or tile would not, and the polychrome on the walls is fresh-looking and glowing. The Stations of the Cross are large, ornate, and impassioned, and the shrines to various saints each stand in a pool of morning sunlight, their votive lights bright in their little ruby-colored glasses, unlit ones neatly ready to embody the prayers of the faithful.

Plaques: in memory of former wardens, of soldiers, of children, of a faithful sexton, of people who kept the faith. The sanctuary was brightly lit, and it looked the way heaven looks in Scripture: gold and cut stones; lustrous snowy-white embroidered silk hangings; autumn leaves red as jewels adorned the altar. I inhaled the special smell of a living church, of generations of candles and forgotten clouds of incense, of old hymnals and waiting wine, of polish on beloved wood.

For All Saints', a procession: around the church, slowly, the congregation falling into line, walking, singing, the thurible sending sweet smoke to linger in the uppermost reaches of the vaulted ceiling. We began: ancient words, new tunes to ancient songs.

I was the preacher. The pulpit is of beautifully carved wood and very high, far above the heads of my hearers. I like that more than one might expect: the people need not look at the preacher if they don't wish to. They may think their own thoughts, allow God to speak to them, either through the sermon or in spite of it. The sermon is not the most important part of such a service: the Mass is a whole, and the climax of it is the Body and Blood of Christ, given and received.

Can all those things that the church building—with its holiness, its airy height, its sweet smells and whispers of memory—reveals to us about God be put into words? Can something be said that will take what we have inside these walls out with us into the street afterward, to walk with us through the week? I began to speak.

I thought I had sped by the World Trade Center site in my car unscathed, but I had not. We read the passage from Revelation that was read so often in churches in those days, not because it was the one assigned as the lectionary reading but because so many preachers chose it instinctively. It is the reading in which John the Divine sees a heaven in which God wipes away every tear from the eyes of those who have been through the great tribulation: "They shall hunger no more, neither thirst any more; the sun shall not strike them, nor any scorching heat." I remembered them, those who fell and died, those lost in that hot mountain of rubble and dust. People in this neighborhood could see the towers as they burned and fell. These quiet streets filled with that dust when the wind turned in those first days a year ago. As in every church in this city, people in this congregation had lost dear ones.

When God wipes away every tear, the moment of suffering is over. This happens right away: right from the moment of death they are in heaven. We are haunted by our sense that they are impaled forever on a moment of terror and pain. It is not so. That is over. Was over immediately. Their new eyes opened into a new world, right away. New, and completely good.

They see us. They see what God sees, and so they see us. They also see that we cannot move quite so quickly, that our hearts are still broken.

Ora pro nobis.

It's Never Better Not to Know

Today is election day. In the first South African election after the ending of Apartheid, some people waited in line for more than a day to cast their ballots. One old woman told a reporter that she didn't mind it at all—she had waited more than eighty years for this day, and a few more hours were fine with her.

The election in the Philippines, which toppled the Marcos regime, was counted in the usual way: old-fashioned, wooden ballot boxes. I remember the *Times* front page that day: men with smiles as big as their whole faces, passing the heavy boxes hand to hand on their way to be counted, as if they were light as feathers. They had waited so long. My husband wept when he saw it.

Everyone in Iraq voted this year, we read. A one hundred per cent turnout. Not much tension in Iraq around the results of the election, but that's some turnout, all right.

We'll hit about forty percent, in this mid-term election. I imagine more of us will shop than vote—lots of sales on election day. A columnist in the *Times* suggested that schools and stores and businesses, theaters and sports arenas all close on election day, that we simply eliminate anything to do other than vote. Wonder if that would work.

Of course not. People would just shop online.

I have never understood why we're not ashamed of this. People caught in the eye of the roving reporter's camera usually snarl something about politicians' being all alike, or not liking any of them. An extraordinary number report never having voted. Then we wonder why our public figures are cynical and self-protective. It's because we elect them, those of us who vote and those of us who don't, *elect* them, in one way or another. They resemble us. They *are* us.

In ancient Israel, the king was understood to be appointed by God. Elected officials still take their oaths of office on a Bible, although they don't have to anymore, if their beliefs preclude it. The idea that God blesses human politics is ancient but still alive.

Nobody *has* to live a thoughtful life. Nobody *has* to look up at the sky in wonder. Nobody *has* to bestir himself in the service of his fellows. They're not going to come after us and *make* us do these things. They're not going to *make* us vote, as they did in Iraq a couple of weeks ago.

But to choose *not* to know, to choose *not* to participate. To walk right past beauty and decide not to marvel at it. To look love squarely in the face and decide not to respond. To toss away the gift of freedom as if it were an empty cigarette wrapper. To choose ignorance and apathy instead of engagement.

I just don't get it.

An Important Visit

Q was up and out yesterday; he could not linger. An important engagement summoned him to Campbell School: lunch with a second-grade class.

An escort team met him. They took his coat and beret. They may not have seen a man in a beret before: Q is an interesting visitor. With his "handlers," Q made a tour of the school, noting points of interest along the way. One of the points of interest was our friend Mary Jones, escorted in the opposite direction by another set of small tour guides. The two visiting dignitaries acknowledged one another, but there was little opportunity to chat: it was time to go to the cafeteria for breakfast: juice and sweet breads provided by parents.

He observed a class about the parts of speech; it was Q's introduction to MadLibs, in which you pull adjectives and nouns and verbs out of the air and then insert them absurdly into a prefab story. My kids loved MadLibs.

Q got a chance to talk about himself. He told them about teaching in Turkey, about the Turkish language, about traveling there fifty years ago on a steamship. He told them about living in Germany, about studying in France and England, about being in the army. One little girl introduced herself as "Skye." Q told her about bicycling around the Isle of Skye when he was young. When he talked about Italy, three children identified themselves as Italian-American. He talked about being an English professor. One little boy raised his hand; "My father had you as a teacher at Rutgers," he said importantly. Nobody could trump that one.

They could ask questions of their highly educated and well-traveled visitor. The questions?

What's your favorite color? "Purple," he said, pointing to his shirt and referencing our purple house, a local oddity which a number of them knew.

What's your favorite food? "Tomatoes," he said, and they talked a little about his vegetable garden.

Do you have any pets? He struggled to capture What's-Her-Name in words, which really can't be done. You have to be there.

How old are you? The answer, roughly ten times their own ages, seemed not to faze them.

Q says that on Thursdays they do poetry. He's thinking of some poems that he might bring them. They will like the poetry; he's got some good ones for people that age. He has always loved words at play with one another. He chooses Robert Frost: "Stopping by Woods on a Snowy Evening."

Perhaps Q is really a second grader, too, a person who has not yet learned to be jaded, someone who doesn't yet know that you're not supposed to be excited and curious. Yesterday, he was among his own. Nobody in the class rolled her eyes and clicked her tongue against her teeth in bored forbearance. That will come later.

For now, they just asked about Egypt and what it's like, and if he had any pictures of the pyramids.

No Shame in Sadness

Depressed people are often ashamed of being depressed. Depressed *religious* people are even more ashamed—we feel such a responsibility to be serene. We think we've let God down. Our faith must be lacking, we think, or surely we'd feel the love of God.

Despair is the great unforgivable sin, we have been told since before we knew what despair was. Suicide is a mortal sin, we were taught. You go to hell for it—BOOM, like *that,* we were taught.

Sometimes I hear the bleak accents of depression in people who come to me for spiritual direction. Sometimes, when I first suggest that their problem may be depression, they recoil, as if I had accused them of a crime. Or as if I were brushing off the concrete issues that hurt them as not real, "all in your head." As if something involving your head couldn't also involve real spiritual issues—hmmn. But, of course, it looks that way to them. They don't want to be depressed. Depressed people are *ashamed* of being depressed.

How odd.

I want them to know they needn't be ashamed. I always make sure I self-identify judiciously—I want them to know that I have firsthand experience of depression and its ravages. That being in treatment for it has not caused me to lose my faith or my capacity to feel things or think clearly or get mad or to become a smiling zombie. That acknowledging its existence is not faithless or cowardly. On the contrary, it is brave.

Our souls are not disconnected from our minds. Or from our bodies. Or from our environment. We can't decide to ignore any of these and expect to be at peace. We are all of a piece with ourselves, and it is not for us to decide how we are to be made—we arrive here made as we are.

Sometimes part of my responsibility is to help people get up the courage to begin seeing a therapist. This can be very hard for them; I've lost track of how many people have said something like, "I can't go to a psychiatrist. I just can't. It would be admitting I don't have faith in God to heal me." This conviction somehow doesn't apply to endocrinologists or osteopaths. Just shrinks. Just those whose specialty comes perilously close to the human soul, and dares to expose its secret sorrows to the light.

So some peoples' pain can be greatly eased by seeing a mental health professional, and I help them get there. They may need to begin taking medication, and they probably will feel very guilty about *that* need—guilty, again, in a way they never would about taking insulin or blood pressure medicine.

But shrink or no, medication or no, they usually also continue to see a spiritual director. They continue to have spiritual issues, continue to be people whose experience expresses itself in the language of a faith tradition, people for whom religious language is not quaint, but current and alive. They have a spiritual home, and they long to go back there. We help them stay connected to it until they're well enough to make the trip.

They may bear a burden their secular fellow sufferers do not bear: the church has sometimes done more harm than good to those in despair. But they also have resources of community, of ritual, of tradition and spirituality available to them that are found only within a matrix of faith. Each is unique: there are many ways of being faithful, and many ways of being depressed.

And many joys to be tasted, in heaven and on earth.

I Can Do This

"Are you guys okay?" read the subject line in the email I sent south to Mark and Shari. The radio described the tornado that swept through Alabama. I'm hazy at best about geography: "Was it near you?"

"We're fine," Mark wrote back. "It was to the west of us." He knew something was up somewhere, though, when the air got funny and the temperature was over eighty. This one was bad.

It wasn't to the west of a lot of people—it was right there. Thirty-five people in six states died, and more than two hundred were injured. The only school in the little town of Carbon Hill, Alabama, was destroyed—and their high school burned down last year, so all the students had been crowded into the middle school. And now there's no school.

"Well, we're the Volunteer State, you know," a man from Tennessee said to an interviewer. Tennessee lost the most people. "We're all just doing what we have to do to take care of people."

I used to know all the nicknames of the states: Connecticut—the Nutmeg State; Maryland—the Free State; California—the Golden State; New York—the Empire State; New Jersey—the Garden State. I had forgotten all about the Volunteer State. But they didn't: it helped them to think about this self-identification as they collected bottled water and trays of food, clean used blue jeans and sneakers and T-shirts, folding cots, extra sheets and blankets, as they opened up churches and helped each other dig through ruined houses, trying to salvage something. *We'll get it done. We're the Volunteer State.*

We don't know what lies within our capability until we are called upon to dig deep for it. That's when we understand that who we are has a lot to do with what we can do. *I can do this: I'm Joe Anderson's son.*

I can do this: I'm a marine. I can do this: once a nurse, always a nurse. I can do this: I'm a grandmother. I can do this. We borrow the strength of the community to which we belong, add it to our own. By myself, I may not be very potent—but I am not *by* myself, am I? I'm related. I have a history of courage and competence, my own and that of others, upon which to draw.

Whose son or daughter are you? Whose brother, whose sister? Whose friend? Is that a legacy of hope or discouragement? Could be either one. Usually, it's a little of both. To whom are you related? What connection gives you strength?

I can do this. I'm a child of God. Not everything the children of God do is a success. But God is the one who brings possibility out of futility, good out of evil, life out of death. We can do this life, with all its terrible reversals of fortune. We can do it because of who we are.

Addicted to Our Enemies

Out of the corner of my eye, a sight that made me stop in my tracks: a pigeon with two heads and four legs. Right there on upper Broadway. It hopped along the sidewalk unevenly, zigzagging this way and that as it went, but it made progress. Lights! Camera! Everybody, stop and look! Veterinary history in the making!

Except it wasn't a two-headed, four-legged pigeon. It was just two pigeons fighting. Breast to breast, their heads pressed together, they shoved against each other and tried to peck, first one and then the other gaining brief advantage.

At issue was a sodden crust of pizza. Well on its way to becoming an amorphous paste of flour, the pizza was, nevertheless, hotly defended by the lighter-colored and slightly larger of the two birds. He disentangled himself from the embrace of the other bird and arranged himself in front of the prize, between it and his rival, dancing a stiff little two-step back and forth: *Don't even think of coming near this pizza crust, Jack.*

The other bird had begun to ignore him and eat other crumbs of pizza, and still he danced. All around him birds were eating pizza, but he was eating nothing. He was too busy defending what he had. He continued to dance his threat as I peeled myself away, after five minutes of watching, and walked on. For all I know, he is dancing still.

Everybody has anger. Everybody must stand up for himself. We all have the right to protect our own interests. But we are not well served by *becoming* our anger, our self-protection, our self-defense. It can take us over. Aggression is energizing—it feels good. We can become addicted to it.

And it joins us to the very one we seek to vanquish. The two birds were so enmeshed that I thought they were one bird, at first. It was like

Dante's Hell: you spend eternity bound together face to face with the one against whom you raged on earth, and you will never escape. I begin by trying to eliminate my enemy; I end by being unable ever to escape him.

The composite bird wasn't a very good walker. It hopped and jerked along, making but slow progress along the sidewalk. We are inefficient if all our energy is devoted to a project for which it is not intended. Maybe we can do it, and maybe we can sustain it, but we'll walk funny.

The bird obsessed with fighting wasn't a very good fighter. Nor was he a very effective bird—he appeared willing to starve to death in order to defeat his foe, never to eat again as long as he could prevent the other bird from eating. There's got to be more to life.

Fear of Failing

A rich man goes away and leaves his servants in charge of things. He treats each one differently: to one he gives five talents, to another two, and the last servant gets one. The two with the higher amount increase what they were given and are rewarded accordingly when the boss gets back. The last one is afraid of losing his, and so he hides it in the ground. He ends up having a very bad day.

How cool: they had a coin called a "talent." A talent was about 6,000 drachmas, back when a drachma meant something—the last time I was in Greece, 6,000 drachmas equalled a dollar or two. So the rich man left his people his wealth: talents. Granted, this is a pun that works only in English. But it works very well, indeed.

Two of the servants will take a risk. The third one won't. He won't act unless he can be assured he will not fail. "Master," he said, "I knew you were a hard man, so I was afraid, and I went and hid your talent in the ground."

But nobody can be assured of not failing. All we have are our talents. And if we're afraid of using them, pretty soon we won't have them, either. They're like muscles: they'll atrophy from lack of use.

No art is created except upon a mound of failed art. You practice and practice and practice, and your first efforts aren't very good. But you don't stop. You cross out and rewrite, you paint over, you try again until you get it right. You're patient with yourself, but not lax. It takes time and humility to create. If I think I have to do it perfectly the first time, I never get anywhere. And if I stop with my first effort and say that's the best I'm ever going to do, I'm settling for an untruth. I don't *know* yet what is the best I can do. I haven't tried.

It isn't laziness, usually, that keeps us from achieving all we want to achieve. It's fear. Fear of failure. Fear of punishment for doing something wrong, years after anybody ever punished us for anything. Fear of looking foolish. It stops us in our tracks. Out of this fear, we end up doing nothing at all.

It helps me to get unstuck when I remember that, in this story, the talents don't really belong to any of those servants. They belong to the rich man. My talents aren't just mine. I didn't give them to myself. They came from God. And so they have God's imprint on them—they show forth the creator. My talents are like seeds: they carry within themselves God's tendency toward growth. They are part of God's fruitfulness. Give them even a little water and sun, cultivate them even a little, and they'll grow. It's how they're made.

Stuck? Afraid to begin? Afraid to make a change because it might be the wrong one? Afraid you might not succeed? Acknowledge your fear and start anyway, and start small. Do one thing. Change one thing. You don't write a book in a day. You don't build a career in an afternoon. Understand that a journey begins with a step, and continues that way, too—it's just a string of steps. Take one.

If you start and continue, you may fail. You certainly *will* fail, at first. But each failure is a corrective to what your work will become in the future. Failure isn't the ignominious end: it's the patient beginning of your wisdom and skill. It's the primary mechanism of human learning and of all human achievement.

This piece is a contemplation of the Gospel reading for Proper 28, Year A: Matthew 23:14–15, 19–29.

We Gather Together

As of this week, we have purchased enough groceries to get the larger of the two free turkeys on offer at the store. I knew we'd make it.

"Would you be open to using an actual recipe for the turkey this year?" Anna emailed me.

"A recipe? For turkey?" I've never used a recipe for turkey. I didn't know there *were* recipes for turkey. My initial response was one of alarm, but then I remembered that I resolved last year not to be the Great Dictator of Thanksgiving this year. Or ever again.

"Why not?" I wrote back.

"Actually, I have a menu," she replied. "Want to see it?"

A menu? Well, I have a menu, too, I guess. An inner one. The same one I've had for the last fifty years.

"Sure," I typed.

Like a flash, a message came over the Instant Message connection:

> *Turkey w/Herb Butter & Caramelized Onion Gravy*
> *Mashed Potatoes*
> *Sage & Chestnut Stuffing*
> *Haricots Verts w/Lemon Brown Butter*
> *Sweet Potatoes & Roasted Onions w/Rosemary & Parmesan*
> *Brussels Sprouts & Pearl Onions w/Horseradish Cream*
> *Corn Pudding*
> *Cranberry Sauce*
> *Apple Sauce*
> *Your Usual Rolls*
> *Pumpkin Pie, Apple Pie, Mincemeat Pie, and Pecan Pie*
> *Coffee, Tea, and Cider*

"How does that sound?" she typed.

"Wow," I replied. *Wow*, I thought.

Last year I tried to sit up in a chair and direct the food preparations. I couldn't sit up that long. I lay down on the couch and fell asleep, arising only to sign off on the gravy and sit down to eat. Nobody needed me to direct, anyway. My girls knew what they were doing. It was the best Thanksgiving dinner we'd ever had.

This year I *could* do the whole thing myself. But I won't. It would make me tired, and I'm tired of being tired. This will be my first Thanksgiving not involving dinner for 200 at some church or other in a long, long time. St. Clement's Thanksgiving dinner for the neighborhood was legendary, an extravaganza of turkeys and pies, of mountains of salad and gallons of coffee. Volunteers emerged from everywhere, donations piled up like manna from heaven. People who usually didn't get much in the way of fresh things carried away loaves of bread, lovely green acorn squashes, bags of apples, gorgeous large onions, bunches of carrots. There was more than enough. It was wonderful.

This year, it'll be me—the un-dictator—my efficient daughters and granddaughters, and my armed husband with his sharp old carving tools. Q used to carve seven or eight turkeys at St. Clement's; he'll dispatch our free one in nothing flat.

They'll be doing the dinner as usual at St. Clement's, I hear. I'm glad. On the night before Thanksgiving, I'll be thinking of them. Of the mountains of food. Of the guests coming in and sitting down to the feast, of the long tables, warm lights, the shabby room that suddenly looks like heaven itself.

Got an extra turkey? A can of something? A dollar or two? Give 'em a call or visit: 423 West 46th Street, New York City, 10036. And tell them I said hello.

At the Monastery

I'll drive back from Holy Cross late on Saturday night, I thought, so I can get to church easily on Sunday. But Saturday night was rainy and dangerous in West Park, and looked to be so all the way home. I was tired, and not feeling especially well. *I'll get up really early and go tomorrow.*

Just me and the bears this morning at 5 A.M. I didn't *see* any of them, but I always know they're there. No deer, either, up and foraging in the rain. Just me and my suitcase, sliding into a cold car and turning the key.

The retreatants—women from a parish in New Jersey—were still asleep as I turned out of the driveway and headed down the road in the dark. We talked, before turning in, of blessing the hours of slumber, of allowing the mind and the spirit to work on what we had talked about during the day together.

The topic was forgiveness. We talked of things done unto us and things we had done, of those whom we cannot forgive, of not being able to forgive ourselves. We talked of shame, the mute paralysis it imposes on a life, the frozen-ness of shame and the welcome release of repentance, a mature voice that can say *I did this and I wish with all my heart I hadn't done it. I am sorry and will try to make amends.* Repentance can end a story. Shame never can. It just goes on and on.

We talked of praying for someone with whom we are angry, of not using words because we can't always be trusted with words about them. About just learning to coexist with the *name* of the hated person in prayer, of praying the name only—no words, perhaps for a long, long time, until the soul is desensitized to its allergic reaction to an ancient injury that still hurts. It can take a long time. We made a beginning.

And in the midst of such thoughtful talk, such painful reflection, a serene continuo: the Hours of the monastic Office. The round of prayers that never ceases, the certain presence of God in the midst of people contemplating God, of ancient words and tunes, of long silences unbroken by chatter. The prayer of the brothers—who rarely addressed us directly—supported us all the day through and into the nights.

We all grew prettier as the weekend wore on: our lined faces brightened and softened, we laughed more. Talking and sharing and sitting and praying—even about painful things—made us all look younger. I was about seventeen when I left. They're still up there: who knows how young they'll be upon their return.

Live Onstage

Back at St. Clement's after almost a year away—not in my old role as rector but to direct a cabaret show: the lovely and talented PJ Nelson, chanteuse. Her dear friend and tremendously gifted artistic partner Darryl Curry—composer, singer, instantaneous arranger, subtle prompter—at the piano.

I sat in my hidden director's perch way up by the lighting booth and watched PJ's life unfold on the stage. Songs from shows she'd done years ago on Broadway. Songs she'd never done but always wanted to do. A funny pair of songs about being a waitress. A medley of three songs that conjured up for all her close friends in the audience vivid reminders of another of PJ's artistic partners—a man named Lee, dead more than a year now. Her life partner. No, that's not quite what happened: we didn't see *him*. What we saw was her *without* him, her on her own, PJ finding her voice again, a voice from before she met Lee, her whole voice, the voice of her whole life.

But Lee really *was* there. He sat beside me, up in my perch where the audience couldn't see him. I couldn't see him, either, but he was there. Always her toughest critic and biggest fan, he liked the waitress numbers and hated the song from *The Yearling* that he had also hated when he was alive—heaven hasn't mellowed him out on that one yet. He was silent during the three songs about love and loss. I wondered if he felt loss himself, or if he was just visiting ours. I wonder about that a lot.

Lee nodded his head quietly when she sang "Love, Look in My Window" from *Hello, Dolly!* It's about a widow needing to love again. He seemed not to mind that life goes on here among us, that PJ is going on with life—good life, joyful, fulfilling life. That people mourn and heal and continue to mourn, that in the midst of our mourning we are still able to love and be loved, that we sample joy and sorrow all the time, every day, mixed together. He seemed to like the idea. It occurred to me that Lee is not separate from the loves that come after him, that the dead *never* are separate. That when we love one another we are loving everything that they have meant, too.

Another singer, an old friend of PJ's, sat in on a couple of numbers, songs that Lee and PJ used to sing together. His voice was different from Lee's, mellower, not nearly so bright—wonderful, but different. Different.

Vi Ward loved the show. She didn't see Lee, either, although he was standing right beside us when we were talking. She was saying that PJ should do that show again in one of the cabaret rooms, that she should take her profession back and give it out to us. That she's really good, and she's ready. Vi knows what she's talking about: she's been in show business since before I was born. She was a vaudevillian, she and her five brothers. The Skilling Sextet, they called themselves, and for decades they traveled all over the country performing. One by one, her brothers have died. "I guess we're the Skilling *Duet* now," her brother Chauncy said to her at their brother's funeral, and a few years later he was gone, too. So now Vi is a solo act. And doing plays and making movies, still.

PJ sat on the stage, collecting compliments and bouquets and critiquing her own performance—this was good, that was terrible. I told her she was incredibly good. I looked around for Lee to corroborate my review, but he was gone.

The Right Thing in the Wrong Place

Great news from Adelaide in Minnesota: there are hummingbirds in the winter! Not out there—they're not crazy—but they've been seen in Delaware. Delaware is right next door to New Jersey. For all I know, there's a hummingbird asking for directions out in my front yard right now.

Why are they there? The article about it says that a few of them just don't migrate, that they have a different internal clock. Maybe they forget. Or maybe these are just hummingbirds who think outside the box.

Unexpected sights are full of meaning. My father looked up and saw a bagpiper in full Scottish regalia in the supermarket parking lot once. He immediately engaged the piper for a worship service he was planning. He'd been wishing for a piper, and now here was one.

I saw a llama in New York City once, crossing Park Avenue right in front of the old Pan Am building. He appeared to be unaccompanied. None of the New Yorkers crossing the street at the same time appeared to notice the llama. It takes more than that to get their attention.

I saw a group of elephants coming out of Penn Station in a line one morning on my way to work. They all lined up and bowed to me. I bowed back and then went on my way.

Years ago, there was a person named Rollerina who frequented the Village. She was always on skates, and she was always elaborately costumed. I say "she," as Rollerina would have wanted it that way, but Rollerina was actually a young man. During the centennial celebration of the Statue of Liberty, Rollerina whizzed by a restaurant in which I was lunching with friends, costumed as the statue.

I wonder what happened to Rollerina. I have the feeling that she is dead. I wonder whose llama that was, and where it was headed. The elephants are not mysterious: the circus was coming to town. I wonder what the out-of-place hummingbirds are thinking of, if they can be said to think.

I wonder, and I worry about them. There is a reason why usual things are usual: the usual works well in its accustomed setting. Sometimes there's power in the *not* usual: that which takes the familiar and shines a light on it so we see it differently. Nobody ever invented or discovered or created anything by doing the usual thing.

Still, unusualness is not, in itself, a virtue. Being unusual does not, by itself, make you an artist, or a writer, or a leader. Artists and writers, actors, all who create and innovate need to beware of becoming entranced with their own unusualness.

There is nothing especially good about being unwilling ever to do what other people do. That's not art or leadership. It's just protracted adolescence. Not every wheel needs to be reinvented. Most are fine just the way they are: round.

Small World

Tomorrow: apple pies for St. Luke's Holiday Fair. As many as I can make. I must go to Variety Village—the little store beloved of all Metuchen children, where you can get anything in the entire world for hardly any money—and buy some foil pie plates, so I don't have to trust in the purchaser of my pies to send me back my mother's precious old ones. Q needn't park: I'll just run in and out. I know right where the pie plates are there: between the candles and the room deodorizers. Variety Village has a logic all its own.

I am excited about going to the fair. This is the first year in a long time that I am here for it. Before, I was always up to my neck in St. Clement's—no time for such suburban pleasures. But there was a time when I did almost all my Christmas shopping at this fair, and my kids loved it. It is a wondrous event.

"This time, I need your help," Mussafar wrote us from Pakistan. He was our guide in India, the man who led us everywhere, who made an arduous trip easy, who showed us things there we never would have seen with anybody else, who had a solution to everything. He has been a guide for all of his working life, and it has enabled him to give his family a good living.

All this changed abruptly on September 11th, 2001, when the people with the money became afraid to travel, and millions of them canceled travel plans. All the people—guides, hotel workers, restaurant workers, craftsmen—in countries for whom tourism is a major industry have suffered ever since. Mussafar's work went immediately to ten per cent of its former volume. The bombing of the World Trade Center and the Pentagon hurt people far away from either of those places.

Mussafar is a smart and resourceful man. Years ago, he set his younger brothers up in the business of importing the gorgeous textiles of his homeland to America: soft pashmina shawls, in every color God has imagined, fine enough to pull through a wedding ring; embroidered pillows worthy of the India Room; silk table covers; splendidly colored napkins and table runners and bedspreads; wall hangings dyed bright and deep as jewels. Things you would have found among the goods on a biblical caravan, things the Queen of the South would have brought to Solomon, things the Wise Men would have had, things Marco Polo would have brought back to Italy—made in exactly the same way they would have been made then. The two young men are in New York. Did we know a place for them to show their wares?

Ah. Q emailed and made some calls.

I can't wait to see what they bring to the fair.

Oh! Ice and Snow!

Snow! I have been reading emails from the Diocese of Bethlehem about the snow they got, but was suspicious of the weather report promising us the same. Last winter we had less than an inch, maybe less than half an inch: an inconclusive winter if ever there was one. But early, early this morning, I got up and looked out.

In the dark, thick snow at the ends of the branches bent them to the ground. The bamboo all leaned together in a graceful earthward swoop, the whole grove of them, like a well-rehearsed corps de ballet. The picnic table was frosted. The birdbath looked like an ice cream cone: *We must go out there this morning and put the heater in it, so the birds can have water to drink.*

I feel better about the defrosting of the Thanksgiving turkey than I did when I snapped awake in the middle of the night. It is in the pantry, which gets as cold as an outhouse and which we count on as a walk-in refrigerator at Thanksgiving. But our walk-in refrigerator is tied to nature: I have worried about the balmy weather, that the turkey would become a science experiment, a neonatal intensive care unit for baby germs and we would all sicken from them shortly after dinner on Thursday. No. We'll be fine now. There will be no science experiment. It's plenty cold out there.

In Morning Prayer, the church assigns the psalms and the Scripture readings, but I choose, from among the morning prayer canticles suggested in the prayer book for each day of the week, the one for which I'm in the mood. The canticles are poems from Scripture: passages that were just too pretty to be merely spoken, and so are named and sung like songs. This morning I chose the longest one. It is called "A Song of Creation" in the modern prayer book, but it used to be called "The Song of the Three Young Men."

Glorify the Lord, O chill and cold,
   drops of dew and flakes of snow.
Frost and cold, ice and sleet, glorify the Lord,
   praise him and highly exalt him for ever.

You have to get what's happening while they're singing this song, which is really much longer than these couple of verses. For reasons which are somewhat unclear, King Nebuchadnezzar has thrown the three young men—Shadrach, Meshach, and Abednego—into a fiery furnace. They sing a long, long, long, long song of praise to God in there—a really long song, for three guys in a fire. This part of it is clearly to take their minds off the heat.

But they don't burn up. When he has his servants open the oven door to see if the boys are done yet, they're not even singed—and the servant sees a fourth person in there, someone whom nobody saw enter. Very strange. The king is spooked, and quickly repents of his anger.

Millennia later, I light a candle and sing their song to God in my office early on the morning of the first snow. Were there really three young men? Did they really survive all night in a hot furnace? Did they really sing this song? I don't know. I wasn't there.

But is God present in nature? In its journey through time, its seasons and cycles, its life spans and its endings? In the tug of it upon the most sophisticated of us, in the way it stops us in our tracks to gaze upon its beauty, the way it continues to surprise us, even after many, many seasons of snow and ice, of flowers and baby animals? Does it comfort us, sometimes, with its immensity, its independence of us, its grandeur? Does it help us deal with our pain, our own private fires?

Yes. It does those things. This much I know is true.

How Was Your Day?

Watch, therefore, lest he come suddenly and find you asleep.

Mark 13:36

It wouldn't have been hard to find me asleep last night. Although Thanksgiving this year was much less work for me than it's ever been, I was still flattened by the end of it, and went to bed at six in the evening. I stayed there for twelve hours. *How can I be so lazy,* I wondered now and then, but I didn't wonder enough to get up and do anything about it. In intermittent snatches of consciousness, I could hear Q telling callers that I was asleep, telling them to call back tomorrow, heard *The Wizard of Oz* on the television in the next room, heard the cats yowling at each other, the dog's toenails clicking like castanets as she trotted down the stairs—heard all these things, and slept on.

Of course, the Gospel lesson for this Sunday isn't really about standing guard at the door of someone else's house. It's about keeping your own house in order, about living each day as if it might be the last, as if you might be held accountable for it that very night.

Did you notice the gift of it?

Did you see its beauty?

Did you weather its trials, seek help with them, look for unexpected strength in unexpected places within you with which to stand up to them?

Did you stop to think about anything, stop to wonder about anything, stop to follow a seeming distraction on a path that led to an unexpected bit of wisdom you would not have found if you had not followed?

Each new day is twenty-four hours long. You sleep from six to eight hours—unless you're me, and then maybe you sleep for twelve hours sometimes. You travel and work, cook and clean, talk and listen, read and write. The day, when it is finished, will never come again. It is over. You will have no second chance. You alone decide how much attention you will pay to the gift of your life during the course of it.

So what's in a day? What is the balance of it? A day in which no service is rendered to others is missing something important. So is a day in which no care of the self is exercised. A day in which the television has more lines than you do is a problem. So is one in which not a prayer is said. I could leave this life later today. Will I have done what I could to fill my life with the things that make it complete?

In the end, it is not so much whether a life is long or short that fulfills it. It's not the number of days or the average of days or the sum of days; it's the completeness of each day. Each one new. Each one a chance to change things. Each one a chance to begin again.

This eMo was written in anticipation of the First Sunday of Advent, which begins the new liturgical year and a new cycle of lectionary readings—in this case, Year B. The Gospel reading is Mark 13:(24–32)33–37.

freedom Isn't Everything

Today the world's Anglicans welcome a new Archbishop of Canterbury. He is, by all accounts, among the more brilliant souls to have occupied that position. His selection was the fervent prayer of church liberals and the bad dream of conservatives, but both ends of the spectrum have been surprised by his utterances since his elevation. He won't change everything overnight. The world as we know it didn't end, and a new one begin.

The world doesn't usually end quite that abruptly.

The new mayor of New York was elected in the ashes of the bombing of the World Trade Center. Nobody had much heart for campaigning; the bombing itself happened on the day of the primary election, which then had to be postponed. Serious thought was given in some quarters to extending the term of the incumbent, whose finest hour by far was his presence during the recovery effort at Ground Zero. But no: the primary election was held later, with a voter turnout even more pitiable than usual.

A billionaire—or maybe he's a trillionaire, I don't know—was elected, and people were sure that things would change. He won't be a slave to donation politics, as he financed his own campaign. He'll be beholden to nobody. He knows how to run a business, it was said—who better to peel New York off the mat and put us back in the game?

But the budget tussles that happen every year happened this year, too, and the threat of service cuts happened as usual, too. The mayor has asked to raise taxes. Howls of pain from business leaders: RAISE TAXES!!???! They thought he was one of *them*. And he is.

The recent election in America left the Republican Party in charge of everything. *Ah, at last,* stalwarts say, *now we'll get things done*. They will do well to beware, though: they may be in charge, but they are not alone.

Exercising power is different from the way people think it will be before they have it. In positions of power, you have much responsibility but hardly any freedom. You don't just do what you want to do. You're not a dictator: you lead a community and have a responsibility to the whole of it, not just the friends you came in with. This is not a craven capitulation. It is a fact of leadership. You lead everybody. You care for everybody.

Even in small communities, this is true. Even families. Even couples. *I want to have a love in my life,* we think longingly, *someone to care for me, to listen to me, to meet my needs.* But, unless the listening and need-meeting and caring is reciprocal, that's not a lover: it's a slave. There isn't a free person whose partnership will give you the power to have and do anything you please without a thought to the effect you are having. Your judgment is not the only one operative. There are two people in a couple. And more in a family: even more needs, opinions, passions, rights. Community bumps us up against one another, forces us to take one another into account, pushes us into responsibilities we may not have sought but must fulfill if we are to stay in the relationship.

Being in relationship necessarily limits me. I decide not to be completely free. Only the solitary are completely free. We understand this to be what Christ has done, as well: surrender power to live among the powerless and allow himself to be limited by their limits.

Lovely Tea

I am so glad I was born after people began drinking tea and not before. The Elizabethans drank ale for breakfast: no tea, no coffee. Not sure I would have been up to that.

"You don't smoke?" the dentist asked, looking at my teeth with his mirror. "Tea," I manage to mumble, my mouth full of dental hardware. "Aha," says his assistant. She knew it had to be one or the other, staining the crevices between my teeth. They scrub at them a bit. Tea does stain, all right. Spill some on something white and you can more or less kiss it good-bye. Or you can admit defeat and put the whole thing in the tea, so now you have a nice cream-colored blouse instead of a white one, and what's wrong with that? I've used it to dye napkins and table cloths, to make new things look old onstage, to make white paper look like parchment. I've used it to dye eggs.

You can put a tea bag on a minor burn or an insect bite and it stops hurting. Truth.

Tea reminds me of my dad. We were tea drinkers in the morning, he and I, before my coffee-loving mother was even awake. The modest clatter of the tea things was morning music for me: I would hear it and go downstairs, and there he would be. I had a dream not so long ago that started out that way: he was down in our old kitchen, making the tea and humming, as he used to do. I hurried downstairs, delighted. I knew he was dead, but there he was, just like before, and I could *hear* him! "I didn't know we could hear you! This is wonderful!" I said to him happily, and he looked at me and smiled.

My teas in college ran to the exotic: Lapsang Souchong was a favorite, with its smoky taste—like formaldehyde, my dad said when I insisted he try some. And jasmine, which was like drinking a flower.

And many herbal infusions, too many to remember.

But my days of adventure are over now. I just drink Plain Old Tea, and have for years. And in every cup I remember him, remember the mornings, remember the after-supper cups of tea, remember tea and a little bite of something in the late afternoons, tea and the newspaper late at night.

The Anglican tradition is smart about the senses. It knows that we don't apprehend everything intellectually, that the canvas of our lives is painted in many ways with many things, that smells and tastes and colors, familiar surfaces and postures all play a part in shaping us. They may shape us for good or for ill, but they shape us. We can't ignore them. So we might as well use them, plant symbols of the love of God and the majesty of God everywhere we look, on everything we touch, in everything we smell and see and taste. Candles, incense, lovely cloth, intense colors in windows through which early sun pours. Bread. Wine.

I pour myself another cup of tea. Ah.

Daily Gifts

Each cat goes to his or her own bowl in his or her own location. The dog knows where her bowl is going to be, too, and waits there for me to put it down in front of her. Later on, they circulate and steal from each other a bit, but initially they are conditioned to go where they belong.

The capacity we have for conditioning is a fine thing. It helps us do the things we want to do. Doing something repeatedly, always in the same place in the same way, trains your body to remind your mind and spirit of how to start. You don't have to make up everything from scratch, every time.

I do it with prayer. I turn on the computer and reach for my prayer book while the machine boots up. When I have finished with Morning Prayer, I write my eMo. The eMo is part of the devotional routine. Everything about it is the same every time, and so I feel that something is missing if I haven't prayed and written. For me, that's much better than asking myself, *Well now, what am I in the mood for this morning? What shall I do first?* My answer would likely be, *Nothing. I'm going back to bed.*

A routine can help a prayer block. It can introduce a path, one that becomes increasingly well-trodden, easy to follow. The path can lead me when my heart is so sad or my brain is so tired that neither could lead me out of a paper bag. If I can get my body in its usual chair, pick up my book … if I can start … my feelings can usually catch up not too far down the road.

Same with writing. I do it every day. I may not do it brilliantly every day, but I do it. I may not do it much—maybe it's only a sentence—but I do it. That's why the eMos are daily, just about; they are part of the spiritual exercises I do as a writer in order to write. If I am to be a good writer, I must be an alert and aware human being first: eyes open, able to see what's really there and bring it to life. When I am blocked as writer, I can usually get unblocked if I stop writing and read a bit. I read something I have written in the past. *Hey, that's not bad,* I think as I read, and my anxiety level goes down. Or I revise—tweak things here and there in something else I'm working on, and soon I am on the path again, feeling the usual calm steady-as-she-goes energy that produces words.

All of the just-do-it-every-day things are gifts for us. They're not jobs and obligations. They're things we can do to encourage ourselves, to strengthen and comfort ourselves. Don't take yourself to task because you aren't regular enough. Clocks are regular; bottling machines are regular; people aren't as regular. Just ask God to give you the gift you need, in order for you to be the person you're intended to be, and then sit back and open your prayer book, get on your treadmill, pick up your pen, turn on your computer. Ask for the gift of prayer and work that is meant for you, and soon you will know what it is. And you will do it almost every day, and feel that something is missing on days you don't. It will have become a part of you that you love and cherish, one that makes you grateful every day.

Never Mind Your Legacy

There was more than one unique thing about John the Baptist. Most of them are not things we are likely to take away with us and use—don't look in *Martha Stewart Living* for recipes like "Confit of Locust in a Wild Honey Sauce" any time soon.

But both of the choices for Gospel readings that will be heard in many churches this coming Sunday show us the thing we can learn from John: his extraordinary humility. He looks to be a man who has crucified his ego, learned to set aside the petty jealousies and one-upmanships that punctuate all our days.

And he appears to have set out to do that from the beginning. He sought his humility. Nobody drove him into the wilderness, or forced him to dress like that. It was what he wanted.

When he met Jesus, he knew that Jesus was the Messiah. We have different accounts of that meeting in different Gospels, from one that occurred when they were both in their mothers' wombs (John leapt with joy when his mother Elizabeth met her cousin Mary, we hear, so in this version the two men are also cousins) to others that suggest that they met for the first time as adults. Who knows?

But we do know that, in each of these readings and in several others, John gives place to Jesus. This is all the more striking if they really *are* cousins, as John is the elder of the two, the elder relative to whom deference should be paid in a traditional society. Hierarchy of age and dignity of age matter in the Middle East, and they mattered even more in ancient times. And yet John stands aside, points to Jesus instead of to himself, steers his followers in Jesus' direction, not his own. "He must increase, I must decrease," he says of Jesus, without visible pain or jealousy. He is intent on his message, is John, and his message is repentance to prepare for the Christ; and now here He is. That's it, as far as John is concerned.

We are rather different.

My friend stares into his coffee cup. We see each other seldom, and I have just asked him about work. With some embarrassment, he talks about his supervisor, who is a woman much younger than he is. He doesn't feel that she values what he knows—he's been with that company for almost thirty years. "I'm a team player," he says, "but I'm angry at her all the time. I guess it shows. She doesn't think I know anything worth knowing. Hell, I was with this company when she was in kindergarten." He thinks he may just retire early.

I sympathize. I am frequently shocked by my own petty jealousies, which are much less well-founded than my friend's real pain. I would have thought I'd have outgrown them by now, but no. I am a bundle of whining ego at times. It is all I can do to conceal it so that I can at least appear to be a good person.

John was executed by the state, his career abruptly cut off after a brief period of remarkable and very public success. Nobody stopped it, or appears to have protested in any way that would have saved him. Histories of the time, outside the histories written by the church later on, do not record his death. In that—perhaps only in that—we are like him. We, too, are obscure.

Few of us will become household names, either in our own lives or after them. Our friends and families will miss us powerfully at first, and then their lives will go on. Sometimes they will remember us. In the next generation, there will be no one who remembers.

John managed to become a person who didn't care about his place in history, about his own recognition factor. And what happened? We remember him.

The Gospel reading choices for the Third Sunday of Advent, Year B, are John 1:6–8, 19–28 or John 3:23–30.

Hearts of Space

Ordinarily, the television in our house is only watched on Wednesday nights for *West Wing*, on Friday nights for *Washington Week in Review* and when a BBC production of Jane Austen novel comes on, or a documentary by Ken Burns. We get all our news from the radio.

But now my granddaughters are staying with us for a couple of months. They watch it a lot. They watch horrible rap music shows, but they also watch *Animal Planet*, on which you can see horses giving birth and elephants getting fed. They want to watch Jerry Springer, and sometimes they get away with it, but not if I'm in the room.

And I'm often in the room. Because the television is in my office. Which is why it's 6:43 on a Saturday morning and I'm in here writing. You need quiet. All I have going now, very quietly, is *Hearts of Space*, a radio program of what—I understand—is called "ambient music," meaning soothing, repetitive, broken chords that never lead anywhere. Music you don't have to listen to.

The computer is also here, of course. And I notice a new icon this morning, for something called the Wild Tangent Game Channel. Good Lord. Madeline the Installer was here.

Because of the television's presence, and that of the computer, my office has suddenly become a population center of the household. It is a tiny room, and it is very important to me that it look nice, an uphill battle with my young office-mates around. I spent an hour or so yesterday picking things up—the papers and catalogues get sloshed about with three of us. Now it looks lovely again, and smells nice, too, with an aromatherapy candle burning—not like yesterday, when I had the stool sample of one of the cats here on my desk, waiting to go with her to the veterinarian, ineffectually wrapped in plastic and making its presence unmistakably known.

Hmmn, Hearts of Lack *of Space.*

When they leave, in about a month, the house will be neater, I suppose. And quieter. But it will be less alive. Less running around town, to school and back again, a less-crowded refrigerator, fewer coats on the coat rack, fewer beauty supplies in the bathroom.

I love the swirl and whirl of their presence, even if it makes me tired—and it makes me more tired than it did when my own were teenagers. It occurs to me that I'd rather be tired this way than stately, well-rested ... and alone. People in your life change your life. Sometimes they may cramp your style. But they also warm your heart.

A Christmas Gift

"What would you *do* with a chain saw?" Q asked me as we drove home last night.

I had emailed him a subtle gift hint: "I want a chain saw for Christmas."

I would cut branches off trees, I explained. Then I would cut down the trunks themselves, when we need to take a tree down, eliminating the necessity to bring in expensive tree people to do the job. I would cut notches into the fatter logs in the woodpile, so that then we could split them easily by hand and not have to rent and transport a big heavy log splitter. My chain saw would pay for itself.

He was unconvinced, I could tell. I was full of good cheer as we drove along—odd, since we were coming home from a funeral, but it had been a great funeral—and so I continued to talk about the implications of my request. I had given it some thought.

"I have decided, though, that if you decide you don't want me to have a chain saw, and don't want to buy me one for Christmas, I won't go and buy myself one anyway."

Q was suitably silent, or perhaps he was just stunned: this was a remarkable concession for me, an unheard-of burst of collegiality. My more usual practice is to seek forgiveness instead of permission.

But I had been thinking, putting myself in Q's place, for once. Thinking about how I have worried and complained about his going up on the roof—I oppose it, fearing that he'll fall off and I'll go outside later to find him face down among the geraniums—and how he has agreed not to work up there unless I am home. And how he has stuck to his agreement, even though he does not think my fear is well-founded.

Perhaps it's silly, but I truly am worried when he goes out on the roof. And I thought of that worry, and realized that the chain saw is the same sort of thing: I may think I can handle a chain saw, but if I plunge him into worry each time I do so, maybe it's not worth it. If he felt at all as I feel about his going out on the roof, I wouldn't want to put him through that.

We can do anything we want to do. We don't have to consult anybody else's interests or feelings, ever. We can just do it.

But sometimes it is Christlike *not* to just do it. We wait for One who, we say, emptied himself of his power and utter autonomy to accept the same limitations as beings far beneath him in might and wisdom. He gave up power—eventually, gave up all earthly power, and accepted an earthly death—in a solidarity with us that continues to be the means of our transformation. He accepted weakness to make us one body, coming to us as a baby, whose only power to survive lay in the love of those who cared for him. And sometimes, if we also accept weakness and bend to one another, follow a path other than that mapped only by the worship of our own autonomy, we create the tough, pliant strength of community with one another.

A Geranium Farm Christmas

Now, if you want to see some Christmas lights, you have to go to Fayetteville, Arkansas. I don't know when things started getting out of hand down there, but for years the entire town—the courthouse, every shop, every lamp post, every tree, every home—has been encrusted with a lace of tiny white lights from Thanksgiving until sometime after Christmas (I hope it's Epiphany, although I don't know for sure). It is like a fairy kingdom. Some people fly to Arkansas just to see it.

I was thinking of the lights in Fayetteville out in our front yard yesterday, standing beneath a medium-sized redbud tree with a tangle of white lights in my hands. All the strings worked, I knew, although one of them had a mysterious patch of dead lights at its beginning and live lights at its end: why would that be? I would do something different this year, I told Q: instead of letting the lights twinkle through the leaves of the azaleas and rhododendrons and climb up a pillar, as they usually do, how about we cover the little redbud with them? One small tree, covered with pinpoints of white light. How about that?

It is harder to cover a tree with pinpoints of white light than one would think. I hadn't bothered with a ladder. *I'll just throw these up there*, I told myself; *the tree's not that tall*. Easier said than done: the string of lights would catch on a branch above my head, too high for me to reach but not high enough to give a symmetrical look to the outline of white lights that was taking shape uncertainly. I stretched and reached, bent branches down to release errant strings of lights that had gotten stuck on them in the wrong place, pitched the string up again and again. Eventually, all the lights were used up, and I had a small tree half-covered with lights, looking like the Christmas tree equivalent of Schubert's *Unfinished Symphony*.

"That tree really looks lame," I told Q when he got home. "That's all right; we'll go up on a ladder and even it out," he said.

Up on a ladder! I could have done that. I could have gone around and gotten What's-Her-Name's ladder from the side of the house, where she uses it to climb up to the second floor and startle me at my office window. "Why do you have a ladder leaning against the second story of your house?" my daughter asks. She used to work for the county prosecutor, and her boyfriend is a investigator. She is knowledgeable about crime prevention. "Is that a good idea?"

I tell her that many burglars come from underprivileged backgrounds and haven't had many breaks in life, and here's one. And that the cat uses it to climb up to the second floor. The truth is, we just haven't gotten around to taking it down, and we're thinking of going up there one of these days to clean the gutters anyway. We should probably take it down. I should have used it to put up the lights on the little tree.

Every day, a list: things we will do. Last Saturday, I talked Q into taking me out for coffee so we could put together our list for the day, and we did that. But we don't get to all the things on the lists. And some of the things I do get to, I don't do well enough, so I have to come back and redo them later.

I think I'll get out there and put the lights on the bushes instead, the way we've always done. I will also give some thought to slowing down a little in the tasks I attempt, to counting preparation time as equal in importance to execution time, so that I can actually complete them satisfactorily.

A Christmas Sermon

Christmas will be easy. Funerals will be hard. That's what a new preacher thinks. But the truth is that it's exactly the other way around.

At a funeral, those who mourn are shocked, even if the death was expected. They may be bearing up well, but they are wounded, hungry for hope, spent and bewildered at their loss and, often, at what has led up to it. As long as you don't minimize the loss (say something stupid like "God needed another angel, so he took Francine."), as long as you honor the life as it was lived on earth and point toward its continuation in heaven, they're comforted.

And afterwards, they will say the sermon was better than it really was.

Christmas is different.

Everybody knows the story of it. Many of your hearers know it by heart—the King James Version, with its Shakespearean cadences. Every Christmas card, every dime store crèche, every angel and every sweet Virgin Mary we have ever known or bought or been given comes with us to church on Christmas Eve. There can be little left in the way of sentiment that has not been milked already.

But if the saccharine sentiment of Christmas is over the top, so is the anxiety that comes with Christmas. After all, if even the Son of God couldn't find a room in which to be born and lay his sweet head, how can there be any room in the inn for the likes of me?

I'm afraid about maybe losing my job.

I'm still angry with my mother and here I am, almost fifty years old, for heaven's sake.

I haven't set foot in a church since my divorce, because somebody told me I wasn't allowed to. But, dammit, I just wanted to come tonight,

Christmas Eve; I just wasn't going to sit alone in that little apartment on Christmas Eve like I'm not even a father anymore, and I just hope I don't see anybody I know who might ask me where she is and how the kids are.

She brings her cancer and her alcoholism and her loneliness; he brings his brother's death and his career change; and they kneel beside the manger with everybody else: with angels, with shepherds who don't seem to have bathed recently, with farm animals whose warm breath is visible in the cold night air. I bring my childhood, its dizzy excitement about this night, my inability to fall asleep for all that excitement, all those years ago.

We bring the hopes and fears of all the years. Exactly that.

You stand in the pulpit and look out at the faces. They hold their candles in their hands, with little paper ruffs around the bottom of them to catch the wax so it won't spill on the seat cushions. Some of them you see all the time. Some of them you only see on Christmas. Some of them you can't see at all: it is dark in the church. Something draws them here, something that doesn't usually draw them, a complex combination of loves and longings. You may not see them again for a whole year, or ever. You must speak in a way that pierces the armor of their despair, that hushes the rush of their excitement, that counters the numbing ease of familiarity. You clear your throat.

And you realize that a Christmas sermon isn't hard to preach because of *them*. It's hard to preach because of *you*. They are here for something that reaches far beyond anything you might say. Every candle, every bough of evergreen and sprig of holly, every carol, every statue and altar hanging and choir singer, everything that makes this worship beautiful is part of how God cares for their battered spirits, striking through everything that has happened in this sad old world to touch their hearts. You stand to preach and realize that your words may not matter as much to anybody else as they do to you. They will go home and say that the service was just lovely, even it they don't remember a thing you said.

You want to delight them. You want your words to be as beautiful as the altar, as fine as the fair linen, as brilliant as the candles, as lovely as the anthem the choir sings. You want it to be spectacular. Truth to tell, you want to be spectacular yourself.

Then you remember the baby on a bed of straw, and his parents. How far from perfection the first Christmas was. How full of fear and misunderstanding it was, how rough, how thoroughly unspectacular. The church service is beautiful, and as elegant as everyone involved can make it. But it must not cover up that long-ago fear, that roughness. For it is in those things that we connect with Christ every day. The evergreens will go out on the curb for pickup, the candle wax will be cleaned off the seat cushions, where it will spill in spite of the little paper ruffs. The poinsettias will grow spindly and drop their gorgeous red leaves, and in three weeks somebody will get sick of looking at them and throw them out. It will not be Christmas anymore.

But Christ will not depart from us. He came into a life like ours, with sorrows and joys like ours. And he will never leave.

No Crib for a Bed

"What did you sleep on?" one of the kids asked on Christmas morning, when Q and I returned from spending Christmas Eve at the convent. I suppose she was thinking in terms of a bed of nails, perhaps, or the bare floor.

"Oh, we had a real bed," I said. "In fact, we had a nice bed in which we could sleep together." There is a pull-out couch in the room where the sisters put bishops when they come to stay, and it has the most comfortable mattress of any such piece of furniture I've ever encountered.

The midnight service at the Community of the Holy Spirit was lovely and solemn. We had music from everywhere: music composed by Sr. Élise, music from other parts of the world, old music from England, the music of drums, the music of handbells, as much fun to watch as they are to hear: the ringers twirl their bells slowly at the end of a song, so as to enhance the reverberation, a stately dance of wrists that I would like to watch over and over again. At the close of the service, incense still hanging in the air, we went down to the refectory in silence and had a midnight snack of cocoa and crackers. It was good to sit in the quiet with no sound but the click of pottery mugs against the table, sipping the warm chocolate sweetness. To be silent instead of riotous after Mass was wonderful: it continued the feast begun in the chapel, incarnated the meaning of it: henceforth, nothing is profane. God-With-Us is with us in refectory, office cubicle, kitchen, on the highway, in the store.

This changed a bit the next day. We had a carol sing after Morning Prayer, and then sang "The Friendly Beasts" all the way down the stairs to breakfast. Three sisters appeared in antlers. Sr. Mary Elizabeth had made three wonderful big loaves of sweet bread, fragrant and studded with golden raisins. More carols: "Bring a Torch, Jeannette, Isabela,"

"Patapan"—songs I hadn't sung in years. "'Friendly Beasts' again," someone cried, "This time with animal noises!" and we were off, sisters offering remarkably accurate camel noises, donkey brays, the moos of cows, baas of sheep. I did a dove cooing. In the animal free-for-all at the end, it was Noah's Ark: brays, baas, coos, chirps, camel honks, all at once.

"And to think we do it all without alcohol," Sr. Élise observed quietly.

Off down the highway for home, to welcome wanderers dividing their time between our family and boyfriends' families. We returned to the news that the dog had fallen down the back steps, they were so slippery. I've never known a dog to fall down any steps, so you know it was hazardous. For the rest of the day, I took her out the front door by her collar, and helped her walk down.

The weather delayed dinner, but not seriously: the mashed potatoes ran out by the time the last shift made it in out of the snow, and so they had hot roast beef sandwiches with gravy instead. I made four plum puddings; we ate half of one. I must give some thought to disposing of the rest. It's not everyone's dessert, but we loved it: Q set it on fire with brandy three or four times, just so we could have the thrill of seeing it.

The snow continued to fall. And, at the end, the weather was too bad for anyone but our old friend Greg to make it home safely—he just lives here in town. And so we had even more people, people the cats hadn't even met yet, people on every couch, in every bed. This troubled the cats, who are used to an abundance of sleeping surfaces from which to choose, and they fought each other over nothing all night.

In an early American painting of the Peaceable Kingdom, the lion is shown lying down with the lamb, as it says in the Bible. Other traditional animal enemies stand happily together, and a child stands with them. He is oddly-shaped: these painters were self-taught. In the distance, you can see William Penn greeting a group of Native Americans with an expansive gesture of one arm. It is a vision, rather than a depiction, of peace—unrealized then, unrealized today. God-With-Us hasn't finished with us yet, and the joyful end of things is not very visible in the sorrows of the present.

At the convent, we had a bed. Here, we ended up sleeping on the floor last night, with the two girls on the couches. "It'll be like a slumber party," I tell them. I've always liked sleeping on the floor, but now my arthritis makes it less comfortable than it used to be, and I was troubled with pain in the night. Perhaps my floor-sleeping days are over.

The dog looked at me, suggesting with her brown eyes that it was time to go outside. I prepared to take her down the stairs, but by this morning she had thought it through: instead of stepping down at all, she simply soared out into space, clearing all four steps in one bound, and scampered off into the snow.

Merry Christmas. God is with us, but this still isn't heaven. Until then, here's a tip or two: when the potatoes are gone, eat bread; set the pudding on fire more than once; if you must be silent in the night, make sure you make a racket when you have a chance; don't forget to wear your antlers at appropriate times.

And if you're scared of falling down the steps, jump.

Midnight Snack

The Great Pantry of Life: you can make something nutritious out of everything that's in there. If you know how.

So what can be made out of pain? I wondered in the wee hours. I must have slept crooked or something: the pain I always have in my right leg was being especially assertive. I writhed quietly, trying to ease it without waking Q, and finally gave up and came in here to write.

So, good: that's one thing. Pain makes people get up and write.

And it can make people pray, too, although we seem to need a reminder—I can endure a large amount of pain with very grim determination before I remember that I could be using it as a way to pray, that I can offer it to God, as a child offers a parent his broken toy. *Fix this. Help me. Help me bear it. Help me relax.* One would think I would get to this step early on, that it would occur to me first, after all this time, but no: I seem to need a solitary walk of some length, through a puddle or two of intense self-pity, before I can turn to God.

And then, when I finally do remember to pray my pain, my prayer has a strange life: it begins with requests and very soon becomes contemplation of God's goodness and love for me. I start out wanting deliverance from my pain and end up just sitting with Christ, imagining the glory of God, feeling the flutter of the Holy Spirit. It reminds me of childhood hurts and how they were healed: I would come in with a skinned knee or a bee sting to get first aid from my mother in the form of a kiss. I don't know why this always worked: kisses don't banish pain. But they make it better.

Where does the pain go? The answer is that it's still there, but that I have gone somewhere else, come into my experience of my own pain through another door. In the topology of prayer, I have folded back on myself and exposed a new surface to God. That's the best I can do by way of explanation, and I am the first to admit it's not very good.

You almost have to have chronic pain in order to practice this. Acute pain—the sudden onset of pain intended to alert the body that something is dangerously wrong and needs immediate attention—doesn't give you enough time. Rarely do you get beyond *Help. Fix. Please.*

But when pain is a constant unwelcome guest, you have time. You run through your repertory of pain-reducing tricks and exhaust them all. You're left with yourself and your pain, and then, finally, you give up. And then God shows you love, and at last you're not working so hard on your pain that you don't notice God's love, and you can gaze at it for the rest of the night and not tire of it, until sleep comes for you.

How does one do this? What is the technique? I wish I could set forth the steps, but what I have described is as technical as I can be. Try everything. Notice that it hasn't worked. Notice that God has been watching and loving you the whole time. Notice that love. Notice it more. Forget yourself in it.

A child with a skinned knee is distracted by a kiss. God's love will do no less.

The Prison of Desire

There is no tasteful way to describe our current problem, so I'll just be direct: Gypsy's in heat. She began to yowl four days ago, and has been monumentally uncomfortable—and, hence, a colossal pain—ever since. I wish I could describe the sound to you: it begins as a guttural growl and ascends in pitch, becoming a protracted wail so rough that I can feel the nodes forming on her vocal cords. Sometimes—I swear I'm not making this up—she adds an "n" at the beginning, so that she is saying the word "no."

But she really means "YES!!!NOW!!!ANYBODY!!!QUICK!!!"

She creeps around the house in a crouchy slink, stopping to rub her head on every surface she can find, so as to leave her scent there in case a suitor should happen by. But the only males in the house are Q, who sympathizes but is already married, and Simba, who has long ago forgotten what all the fuss is about. So have the other female cats: Kate snaps and hisses at poor Gypsy, while What's-Her-Name regards her with an idle curiosity tinged with contempt. They have never experienced heat themselves, and don't know what it's like.

"Did you know that porpoises and human beings are the only species that enjoy sex?" Rosie asks at dinner. No, we didn't know. This is what you learn on *Animal Planet*. Q wonders if we shouldn't discontinue cable television; if we did, though, where would we ever hear useful information like this? "The boy cats have spines on their winkies that hurt the female."

Good Lord. I don't even want to think about that.

I watch Gypsy pace and howl, and wonder what it is to yearn so profoundly for something one doesn't even like. Wonder how it has come to be that the survival of the feline race depends on an act that is unpleasant to half of it. Wonder why it is that pain and annoyance are built into their reproductive process?

Of course, pain and annoyance are built into ours, too, as well as into lots of the other things we do besides have babies. We are powerfully motivated by discomfort and lack of balance: they make us want to straighten things out, to get back into synch. But we need to know, first, what it is to be *in* balance in the first place, to be out of pain. We need some idea of how we can achieve that which we lack and miss so. Somewhere along the line, we must have experienced rightness in order to long for it powerfully enough to do something about it. Otherwise, we won't think it possible to live in another way. We will just sit in the prison of it, not knowing there was another way to live.

Gypsy's in prison now. She has kept the whole house awake at night for four days, and we need our sleep. So she's in the little bathroom downstairs, a tiny, unheated space that confines her overnight. Interestingly, she has quieted in there. Maybe her pacing isn't the best thing for her: maybe being still helps her more. Maybe an actual physical prison lessens the heavy weight of her hormonal and spiritual one. Maybe it forces her to stop, to face the fact that she isn't getting what she feels impelled to have, to cease searching for it everywhere.

Her troubles will be over on Thursday, when she goes into a surgery that will render all this a distant memory. For now, though, she's one miserable animal. When she has forgotten, though, I will remember. I will remember that she wanted something she didn't really like, and looked for it in places where it wasn't anywhere in sight. I will remember that a prison seemed to have helped her. I will look into her ageless green eyes, and it will be, for a moment, like looking into a mirror.

Ask for Help

There is a logical connection between the Feast of the Holy Name, which occurs on January 1, and the secular custom of making resolutions for the New Year. The Hebrew name "Jesus" means "God saves." Those of us who have made New Year's resolutions and broken them with discouraging promptness know that the act of resolving is not, by itself, enough to change us. We lack the power to change ourselves. We require a power beyond ourselves in order to change entrenched behaviors.

And we have such a power. We are not alone in our struggle to become, more and more, the men and women God would have us be.

HOW TO CALL ON GOD FOR HELP

☐ **Recognize that you need it.** Admit that doing the same thing the same way, over and over again, hasn't produced different results yet and probably won't.

☐ **Ask God for help.** Do this every day, every time you pray, from grace before meals to the Holy Eucharist and everything in between. Keep it short and simple: *Help me eat only what I need. Help me wake up early enough not to be frantic. Help me to drive carefully. Help me not to smoke.* But do it every time you pray, without fail. If possible, do it out loud, even if you are alone. Things we say out loud feel more real to us. And use the Name of Jesus frequently. Remember what it means: we don't have to save ourselves—God saves us.

☐ **Observe and learn from the wisdom of the 12-step tradition.** You don't have to be an alcoholic to use the steps. Read through the twelve steps, substituting the thing you want to change for "alcohol" as you read. You can find them listed at:

www.12steps.org/Brochure/12step/12steps.htm

Does it seem to fit? Is this something you can use? Indeed, is there a 12-step group that brings together others who are trying to change the same thing you want to change? Consider attending several meetings, and listen with an open mind.

☐ **Resist negativity about the thing you're trying to change.** Have scolding and berating yourself about it really helped you to do this differently up until now? Probably not, or you wouldn't still have the problem! This time, try a positive and loving approach to yourself, seeing and loving yourself as God sees and loves you. This whole project, after all, is only for your joy and health. It is nothing but good. Don't turn it into some kind of punishment.

☐ **Give yourself treats.** You have a habit that is not helpful to you, but it has helped you get through life. A bitter, martyred feeling of self-denial does not. Develop alternative things that will reward you but won't hurt you: a lovely hot bath, a cup of nice tea, a magazine article you've been saving to read. Tell yourself often what a good thing you're doing, how brave you are to be doing it. Give yourself compliments! Be liberal with your rewards: they help you stay on the road you've chosen by reminding you of God's love.

☐ **Acknowledge that this is hard.** Do not compare yourself with other people for whom your chosen task is not hard.

☐ **Consecrate yourself to your chosen task.** Consider attending church on some day you don't usually go to church, as a special way of consecrating your intention. Silently or aloud, ask the prayers of the congregation for you and your good work. Receive the church's sacrament of healing with laying on of hands if it is offered. The saving Name of

Jesus isn't just private and individual. It works through the congregation as well.

☐ **Tell people who care about you what you're doing.** Ask for their prayers and support. Tell the clergy, and ask for their prayers on a consistent basis.

☐ **Conduct a personal review of each day at its end.** Each of these practices is an ongoing one. We keep doing each of them, again and again. How did it go today? Where did you win a small victory? Where did you fall down? How can you do things differently next time?

☐ **Plan ahead.** Don't let yourself be ambushed by an opportunity to fall into old ways. Anticipate situations in which you are likely to be tempted, and make plans for how to deal with them. Remember that failing to plan is planning to fail.

Back to Work

Late to my eMo this morning—I was all ready to come in here and get going when I heard a panicked young voice: "I was supposed to get up at five! I have to write a paper!"

Okay. I'm a very nice woman—I didn't mention anything about the fourteen days she's had up until six this morning to write the paper. Not a word. With regret, I left everyone sighing for their eMos until just now, after nine in the morning, the day half over.

Today was also the day Gypsy was supposed to be spayed. I tried wrestling her into her detested cat carrier, finally prevailing by locking together her front and back legs and passing her through its door upside down. She'd been locked in the little bathroom downstairs all morning, while the other cats ate their breakfasts: nothing by mouth, they said. But, in the end, the vet rejected her: her heat hasn't been over long enough. Her inner organs are exhausted and fragile, as are her owners. She might bleed to death during the surgery. The vet doesn't realize how close Gypsy came to being murdered anyway, up howling at all hours of the night these past ten days. Come back in a month, they said. Okay.

I just have time, I think, to crank out the eMo before the dog has to go to the vet, too, for a checkup and a pedicure. Perhaps the cat's delay is just as well: it will give us time to amortize the cost of all this attention over a longer time. Animals seem to like it when you spend a lot of money on them at the vet. It makes them feel cherished. It's the only thing about the vet they like, this chance for you to show you care.

It is an odd school week: only two days long. *Why bother?* I wondered as I drove Rosie to the high school. Nobody wants to go back. We want to stay home and keep Christmas going a little longer. We should all stay home until Twelfth Night. But no: school starts today. Okay.

There's a Standing Committee meeting up at diocesan headquarters this afternoon. That feels odd, too: we're going to be doing what we always do, deliberating on some candidates for priesthood, on some people who have been elected bishop in faraway dioceses, on some churches' sales of property. The usual stuff. Okay.

We press on, into the usual stuff. We have awakened into a new year, and it's feeling pretty much like the old year. We're doing the same things, going to the same places.

This was what it was like in the weeks after the Word became flesh the first time. Things looked much the same—no, they looked *exactly* the same. Most people in the first century lived and died without ever knowing he had come. The crucifixion and resurrection occurred without attracting anyone's attention in the world outside the nascent church. The stream of life went on, and everyone went on with it.

Life goes on. We don't get to choose whether that will be true: it will be true. But we do choose how we will live it, whether or not we will live it as if the Word has become flesh. As if the most mundane things are now sanctified by the use of the Son of God. As if all our work is holy work now, and all our lives, holy lives.

"Christmas comes but once a year," an old poem begins. The incarnation happened once for all, but we need a yearly reminder of its power, and more: Christian feasts are not just reminders. They are, in a strange way, *real*: yearly returns of the wonder of what God has done, actual quickenings of God's activity within us, visits between this life and the larger one to sustain us in a world that wearies us. They bring us, for a moment, closer to something that is always there for us, but which we ordinarily have no time to see or experience.

Is Christ somehow more incarnate at Christmastide than at other times? Of course not. Christ has not moved. It is we who have moved closer. If we will.

Finding Jesus

Many preachers this Sunday will choose between the very slim pickings of stories about the early life of Jesus: the flight into Egypt and the time he ran away. I'm not sure either is one I would have chosen if I had been compiling Jesus stories in the first century. But someone chose them, and *only* them.

They left other stories alone, stories that made the rounds in the early church but didn't make it into the canon of Scripture: tales of precociously performed healings and raisings from the dead, of childish curses, literally and rather frighteningly fulfilled. Tempting as they must have been for some, such things were left alone. We don't read them in church; we have only their shadowy apocryphal half-memory.

The scrapbook-making part of us that wants to hang onto things wants more details. Did Jesus help his dad in the carpentry shop? Did he brush his teeth? What did they have for dinner? Did St. Anne and St. Joachim baby-sit, sometimes, when Mary and Joseph went out? Where, exactly, was their house?

It's a good thing we don't know these things. We'd gild them all, enshrine the ephemera of his days and make them sacraments—we'd have thirty or forty more sacraments and feasts. We'd have the Feast of the First Day of School. The Feast of the Baby Teeth of Our Lord Jesus Christ. The Litany of Household Chores.

It was a bitter cold January morning. It must have been ten or more years ago: I was still at Trinity Church, Wall Street. I was in the bookstore when somebody came to get me: David needed some help. He was a client of John Heuss House, our drop-in center for the mentally ill homeless. He was a large and handsome man, intelligent and well-educated. With his white hair and full beard, he looked like a college professor, and he carried himself with the dignity appropriate to one.

Well, sometimes. At other times, his demons got the better of him. This time he was walking along Rector Street, barefoot and clad only in a white loincloth he had constructed out of a torn sheet. The temperature was down in the single digits.

"Aren't you cold, David?" I asked. "Want to come in, and we'll get something to cover you up a bit?"

David looked at me as if he had not heard, but he stepped into the lobby of Trinity's office building. The security man looked at me inquiringly. I nodded slightly, and he began to dial Heuss House. David leaned toward to me, and spoke with an air of confidentiality.

"I look more like the Lord this way," he said, gesturing at his skimpy attire.

"Ah."

He leaned closer. "I just realized something." He paused importantly.

"You did?"

"Yes." Another pause.

"What's that?"

Closer still. "I'm God."

He did look like Our Lord in his white loincloth, just like the figure of Christ on countless crucifixes—maybe a little old, but very like him. Soon, Joan from Heuss House arrived with a coat and some boots, and she and David set out into the cold, back to Beaver Street.

"Don't tell anybody yet," he said over his shoulder as they left. And I didn't. This is the first time I've mentioned it to anyone.

It was his illness that fastened on dressing like Jesus. Looking like Jesus. Doing what he did. But those who are not ill also want to know: WWJD, people wear woven into bracelets around their wrists. What Would Jesus Do?

Very often, we do not know what he would do. Sometimes, we find a way to assert that he would have done what we would like to do, enlisting him in our various causes as if we really knew. But the sketchiness of biographical material about Our Savior, though it may frustrate our curiosity, also protects us from trivializing his saving work. The very first believers did not choose to focus on what he did because they were so focused on who he was. We know that the first stories they told one another were the stories of his death and resurrection. Tales of his birth and teaching came later.

In its earliest beginnings, the church chose mystery over biography. All our ethics flow from the mystery of our encounter with the risen Christ. Cut off from the mystery, we reduce salvation to a set of rules.

The Gospel reading choices for the Second Sunday after Christmas, Year B, are Matthew 2:13–15, 19–23 or Luke 2:41–52 or Matthew 2:1–12.

The End of the Season

"I don't want you to take the tree down all by yourself," Q said. "The girls should help."

"I don't mind," I said.

"They liked decorating it. They can help with the dirty work."

Actually, I've never thought of taking the tree down as dirty work. It has always been a satisfying task, this bittersweet laying to rest of a lovely household season. Everything must come down today: the Christmas cards on display, the papier-mâché angel, the tree made of pine cones, the Nativity scene that Q had when he was a little boy, with a stable that he made himself. The lights. Stripping the house of these things and packing them away is liturgically slow; I grow wistful as I proceed. It puts me in mind of the shortness of the years, of what they have held. I will be shocked late next Advent, when I will handle again ornaments that, I will feel, I have just put away.

Some of them live in a special box. The paper star Corinna made when she was four, its tinfoil veneer all but disappeared. Her plastic lids on strings, studded with squares of construction paper to look like stained glass: one of them has lost all its construction paper, and I hang a naked lid on the tree every year because I can't bear to throw it away after all its faithful service. Her Popsicle-stick star, beaded with fake pearls from a necklace of mine that broke that year. And a Popsicle-stick Star of David, and a Popsicle-stick cross. The tiny fragile angels my mother had, and the two gorgeous, beaded, ribbon balls she made, shortly before she died. A little Swedish star. Some undistinguished glass ornaments from when I was little, still flecked with the spray snow my brothers and I raised havoc with one Christmas long ago.

More than once, I have sat with a divorcing person and heard the

---

same lament: "He wants half the Christmas ornaments!" This seems to be the unkindest cut of all. It can happen in July, along with the division of everything else: one or the other remembers the Christmas tree, and another piece of life together walks out the door, ripped from its fellows in their special box with its little cardboard compartments, and carried away forever.

The discarded trees line the sidewalk, and have for more than a week: not everybody observes the twelve days. We don't discard ours: Q cuts off the branches and blankets the garden with them, so things can stay a little warmer in the cold. Then he cuts the trunk into little logs and stacks them to dry. In the end, the tree gives every bit of warmth it has: warmth to our hearts first, then to the plants, finally to the fireplace. And its ashes go in the compost. To do it all again.

God-given Uncertainties

The grandchildren and their pets have been with us for almost two months. Soon they will depart for their new home. I can tell that the teens are eager: it has been a bit crowded for them here, and also more than a little old. I imagine their mother is eager to sleep on something other than a couch, although she has not complained.

The cats—theirs and ours—have formed a colony, in their odd way: I come into our bedroom and see two of them asleep on our bed. Most unusual for cats, who usually want to avoid each other. What's-Her-Name, especially, seems to enjoy the companionship of Gypsy, for games of let's-pounce-on-each-other-from-behind-the-door, and of Simba, for meditative peace and quiet. This is the first I've known of What's-Her-Name's being interested in meditation. Clearly, I've underestimated her. She is much more thoughtful than I ever knew. When Gypsy was in heat, catnip was one of the very few things that could distract her. Not wishing to leave anyone out, I sprinkled it gaily on the rug in the hall. Four drunken cats rolled around there together for the better part of an hour. Together! Since when do cats like to be together? Kate alone remains aloof, as always, emerging from her hauteur only long enough to swipe the dog on the nose as she passes.

The dog! Dancer! We will miss her—eager to go outside, eager to be petted, eager to sit in the chair with you as if she were a five-pound Yorkshire terrier instead of a thirty-seven-pound shepherd-blend mutt. Dancer is eager for everything. She makes us laugh every day. I had forgotten how nice it is to have a dog. I would begin a campaign to keep her, if she didn't love her family so completely.

They will be glad of their new home. To make it their own will be exciting. They will live there a long time, I imagine: it will be that home from which the girls move out into adulthood, that home to which they return on holidays, that home that comforts them when they need comforting. That home will be a very lively place for the next ten years or so.

This place will be quiet. A friend writes, musing about leaving her home of forty-five years versus staying put. She makes me think of the same thing. Of ten years from now. Will we be here? Will we be well? What will we be like?

I'm so glad we don't know. Could there be anything worse than having it all programmed for us and knowing it, moving through from one inevitable step to the next, with no uncertainty and no surprise? There is probably nothing as important in our lives as our uncertainties. I begin to think they are God-given.

Life Will Remain a Mystery

Do the Raelians really have two clone babies now? We were suppose to know this week, but the journalist who was going to supervise the tests to find out has become annoyed at the clone-church people and quit. So it could be a while. In the meantime, we are left with our sheep and cow clones. And, I believe, some mice.

The Raelians *do* consider themselves a church: their deities are aliens from outer space, who came to earth and cloned themselves, and that's how the human race began. I guess they would say that the story of Adam and Eve is an account of that cloning: the building of Eve out of a piece of Adam. The making of one human being out of another. I imagine they would apply the same reasoning to the birth of Jesus—this is a cloning, veiled in centuries of legend. I guess they would say that our model of the Trinity is a concealed memory of our cloning forebears: all one, all separate, not the same, but of one Being. Whew!

The nature of religious assertion is such that it can neither be proved nor disproved. I can't prove that aliens didn't come and clone themselves, although I cannot help but feel that I would be thinner if that were so. Nor can I demonstrate the historical or scientific fact of the Resurrection. The Raelians' bursting upon our scene reminds us what religious assertion is for: it isn't just to explain what has been, but to chart the course of what will be, and what we will do. How we will live.

The Raelians represent the latest version of humanity's ancient dream: we will control everything. There will be nothing we did not author, nothing we do not understand. We will not fail. We will not die. We will be perfectly formed, all of us.

Nature will always confound our drive to control and monitor it. The creation is endlessly adaptive. It summons unexpected responses to our manipulations. It feints and dodges, and always wins. An essential freedom characterizes all life, from paramecium to supermodel. Something new can always happen. And we don't know in advance what that will be, or when it will be, or how.

A woman comes for her appointment. Her face is weary and sad. She has just tried for the third time to conceive without results. "We said three times, and now it's three times," she says tonelessly. "I guess this is it. I don't know." She's not trying to be Ruler of the Universe or create the perfect human being. She just wants desperately to be a mommy. Her doctor is the best in the city. She and her husband spent thousands of dollars. They would be wonderful parents. They've now done everything they could, but nature has proved intractable this time. It is a miracle, we say of a birth, and we are right: a breaking into our world of the very power of life. We pray for it and long for it, plan for it and arrange for it as best we can. But we do not rule it. This may be both joy and sorrow, by turns, but it is the truth. We enter life and leave it in ways that are, in the end, not up to us.

"Do you know if it's a boy or a girl?" I ask an expectant mother at church, and she smiles and shakes her head. "We didn't want to know," she says, "We're going to be surprised." I am struck by how many new parents decide to wait and find out the old way, even though they all can know the sex of their babies now.

I'm always a little pleased when I encounter this. "Be it unto me according to Thy will," is how I hear it. They enact a sweet humility in their small decision to allow themselves to be surprised. This attitude at the beginning is good practice for the rest of life. Everything about life is a surprise. And so they wait in faith they didn't know they had, inhabiting the mystery of life for the very sake of the mystery, as well as of the miracle.

Good-byes

"Are you going to miss me, Mamo?" Dancer said, putting her head in my lap.

Corinna talks for Dancer, in a special funny voice that only she can produce. We all love it when she does that. She has captured the dog's artless self-absorption, devout love of her family, secret fears— "That's all right, Mamo, I don't need to have an operation. I'm feeling all better now. You can call the vet and cancel." Her interest in cheese-burgers—"Q forgot to give me cheeseburgers. But never mind, Mamo. That's okay. I'll just starve." Her longing to be petted, her annoyance at the cats—"Can we talk about the cats? There are too many cats here." Her joy at going outside and plotting to get there. One can have a long, long conversation with Dancer through her mommy, almost forgetting that it's all really ventriloquism.

I'm going to miss them all. The unmistakable evidences of the presence of teenagers in a house. Their highs and lows. The transparency of their armor, failing to conceal completely the fearfulness of the first tentative steps of young people setting forth into the world. The chance to support a grown daughter with a lot on her plate. The chance to delight in her again. The chance to take care of her again, after years of living apart—and the delicate task of not taking too *much* care. She is not my baby anymore, and hasn't been for a long time.

We could hardly wait to visit the new house. Q and I got there first. We had no key: we prowled the back yard, looking at the plantings and talking about shade and light. A nice stand of mature irises. A couple of lovely bushes in the back, and two that seem to be signaling some need. Some good trees—Madeline had asked about climbing trees, so she should be aloft in one of them shortly. A couple of roses—too soon to tell who or how they are.

Madeline will take a bus to school now. No more daily rides from us. Rose will probably walk. They'll still forget lunch money and call us, I guess. They'll come over for dinner sometimes.

They walk from room to empty room. Rose's new room has sports car wallpaper—coming down today, I think. Madeline is looking hard at paint chips. The countertop in the kitchen is bright orange: we have a consensus for its replacement at the earliest opportunity. Lots to do. Exciting.

A cat stalks by and throws the dog and me a scornful look over her shoulder. I stroke the dog's beautiful head. Her caramel eyes hold mine. Yes, Dancer. I'm going to miss you a lot.

New York New York

It's a long walk from the E train to the Times Square shuttle. The Port Authority's renovating effort, which has achieved great things elsewhere, hasn't gotten around to the tunnel joining them yet. Long and airless, not as grimy as in years past but no beauty contest winner either, it's a full cross-town block and two uptown blocks underground.

But a couple of days ago, it felt good in there. It was cold outside, and the closeness of the tunnel—which makes you want to die in the summer—felt downright cozy. The people walking in it were more relaxed than usual. It was the weekend.

Rounding the corner to the shuttle, I saw a mime. We have more mimes in New York than one would think, underground or on the street, if weather permits. This one was painted silver and dressed in silvery spaceman clothes. He had a soundtrack with him that played a mechanical whistle-and-whir now and then, and each time it sounded, he changed his position slightly, as if he were mechanical; other than that, he was motionless.

I love and respect mimes, and would have spent some time watching him, but a commotion nearby drew my attention away. Five young men were drumming up an audience for their breakdancing show. They had their marketing spiel down pat, and they spoke it in unison to amplify their voices as they urged us to come closer. They abused the audience with great good humor, and soon a crowd of fifty or more was in danger of blocking traffic in the tunnel. Pedestrians walked through the show with some regularity, unaware of what they were doing until it was too late, and then they had to dodge the cartwheeling, somersaulting, head-spinning—on his head, with no hands!—handstanding, leaping, laughing young men to reach the other side in safety. "I need four divas!" one of the young men shouted, and soon four young women were pulled from the audience, to be lined up with much sexual innuendo and, eventually, leapt over by one of the performers in an incredible display of athleticism.

They collected money—"Just take five dollars out of your wallet and give us the rest"—in large shopping bags. "The more you give, the more we'll have," one said. Cheerfully, they used their audience's fears against them—"Your donation will keep us out of two places: the poor house and *your* house." "Give us five dollars and it will help us pay for college. Give us enough more and we won't have to go!"

We loved them. I forked over five dollars and was rewarded by being called "sweetheart." As the shuttle pulled in, I stopped by the completely eclipsed mime and put a couple of dollars in his box. Poor guy: he can't say thank you, and he can't tell the breakdancers to go away. Mimes don't talk. "Is that a real man?" a woman asked me as I turned to get on the train. "Yup," I said.

No performers at Grand Central. Nothing more on Metro-North to Poughkeepsie. Nothing until I reached the Cathedral Parkway stop on my way home the next day. My favorite busker of all hangs out there. A ruined-looking man in shabby clothes, he once had a voice like that of Johnny Mathis, and once in a while still does. He is a very odd song stylist: "Look at ... (long pause) ... me ... (long pause) ... I'mashelplessasakitten ... (long pause) ... upatree...." He always thanks us for our attention, and reminds us that, as always, we should feel free to dance.

Back in Penn Station, a four-piece jazz ensemble near McDonald's in the Long Island Rail Road concourse is playing "You and the Night and the Music." Upstairs at New Jersey Transit and Amtrak, they're playing a Strauss waltz over the speaker system. Nobody says anything about dancing.

We have Russian violinists. We have Peruvian folk artists. We have alto saxophonists. We have Vietnamese stringed instruments with names I don't know. We have bluegrass bands. We have a black-and-white-painted mime who spends an entire afternoon making a spider web out of string. We have a green Statue-of-Liberty mime. All underground, or in the parks when the weather's better, or on the street. All free for the listening and looking, unless you've got a dollar or a quarter or a dime to give.

I always give them something, if I have money. These are gifted artists. There are easier gigs than street performing. At the end of the show, they gather up the coins and bills people have thrown. I think about them as I ride home, and about a prayer in our prayer book:

> O God, whom saints and angels delight to worship in heaven:
> Be ever present with your servants who seek through art and
> music to perfect the praises offered by your people on earth;
> and grant to them even now glimpses of your beauty, and make
> them worthy at length to behold it unveiled for evermore;
> through Jesus Christ our Lord.

It's a prayer intended for church artists and musicians, not for buskers in the subway stations. But I have always believed that anyone who creates beauty is performing a godly act. So the buskers get the prayer intended for the great organists. It is, after all, New York: If you can make it here, you can make it anywhere.

Not Everyone Is Wired

"Somehow I'm getting three eMos now," the email said. "Could you change my entry in your list?"

My heart sank. Another one. About a month ago, the eMo list grew too large to send from my email program, and so I chopped it up into alphabetical chunks. Now I send it in five chunks. But it seems that some people inhabit more than one chunk—what's *that* about? Their names and their email addresses begin with different letters, I suppose—or it's just a mystery. I read through the hundreds of names until I find the offender, which, within an alphabetical chunk, appears in the order in which it entered the world of eMos. Thus, if your name begins with "C" and you began receiving eMos last summer, you'll be near the top of the Cs. This, I hasten to assure you, is not my idea. It just happens. Another mystery.

The "delete" button begins to look good.

I used to hate these machines. They used to make me cry. I haven't cried over this computer at all—I even miss it when I have to be away. What it can do, what it can help me do—amazing! Whole books submitted over the ether, landing in the inboxes of faraway editors. Thick packets of old eMos lying safely in their virtual filing cabinet, with a reserve floppy disk as a night light, just in case. How it can clean its own room in there, making more space on its desktop, something I've had a hard time doing in real life since my first desk. How it can detect a virus, and quarantine it. How it can play the radio.

How it can create community. The Diocese of Bethlehem chats and jokes with its bishop throughout the day, announcing plans for meetings, canceling them, arguing good-naturedly with one another about the meanings of words and their usefulness, sharing prayer concerns. It is as if they were all just down the hall from one another—a golden thing in a small parish, where there is apt to be no one down the hall, no one else for miles around who shares something of the same joys and sorrows in parish ministry. Colleagues talking about the world and the work they love, and helping one another with that work.

These machines can join many different worlds and make them aware of each other. They can cover us with a light blanket of thought and prayer. We can learn from one another through them.

At the same time, the exciting possibilities they offer us can entrance us, and make us forget something important: as I tap away at the keys this morning, half the people in the world have never made a telephone call. As we—who have these machines, and this software, and this electricity coming out of our walls to power them—get closer and closer with one another through them, we get farther and farther away from the poor.

This is a sorrowful thing. And it is dangerous. Increasingly, many people prefer to live in the eWorld. But, if we stay here, and become comfortable only here, we will create something we do not want: a world in which a privileged minority—defined not by race or ethnicity but by access to virtual communication—insulates itself completely from the needs of those without such access. A sort of eApartheid.

However amazing we become with our machines, however much a part of us they are, however lightning-quick our communication becomes, the central spiritual problem for us remains the one Jesus lifted up: *I was hungry. I was thirsty. I was sick. I was in prison.*

The computer helps us love one another. That is a lovely thing. But the exquisite ease of being with each other in cyberspace may make us unwilling to be with the poor, whom we will not meet there. We may just leave them behind.

How's Work?

"How are your books doing?" someone emails. I never know the answer to that—you don't hear about your sales except once or twice a year, depending on the publisher. The books are the same as people, by and large: some more successful than others, all of them beloved by the person who gave them birth and of occasional mild interest to other people.

Jane Austen published her work anonymously: "*Sense and Sensibility*, by a Lady," "*Pride and Prejudice*, by the author of *Sense and Sensibility*," and so on. Such shyness paid off more than it would today: although it was difficult for her at first to get her works into print, she ended up making money as a writer during her life, and has really cleaned up since then.

Dorothy L. Sayers, when she was unknown, had her friends write letters to newspapers complaining about the heresies in her first book. It worked, demonstrating the truth of the principle that there is no such thing as bad publicity, something we learn today from reality TV.

Amazing: I read today about a television show especially for has-been celebrities—they come on the show and attempt impossible silly tasks, at which they fail. I guess they hope the casting director will see and remember them and they'll get work again. It's hard to imagine that this ever actually happens. I suspect something much sadder is afoot: they get one more chance to be in front of the camera, and are willing to mud-wrestle Tanya Harding to do it.

Most of us will never be household names except in our own households. We'll have to make do without fame and, most of us, without much in the way of fortune as well.

But of course, the real pleasure of doing the work you love is the work itself. I've known hundreds of actors well. Few have been famous ones. All the rest have walked the road of the journeyman, waiting on tables, walking dogs, doing what it takes to stay in the profession they love. Some stay forever—I know a vaudevillian who's still working. Some stay for a season, and then bring what they learn into the rest of lives that unfold in very different ways, in very different places.

Who is to say how your work is going? Only you. Do you enjoy it, at least most of the time? Does it matter to you that it's done well? Do you continue to learn about life through it? It is enough.

Pray for Peace

In Washington this past weekend, a peaceful, immense demonstration against the coming war, numbering in the tens of thousands—thirty? sixty? more? You never really know how many people are out there.

A notice up on the wall in the tiny church where I filled in for a friend yesterday: Prayers for Peace, 9 A.M. on Fridays.

Emails from friends about their children going to Kuwait, their nephews. A quick wedding in upstate New York, followed by hardly any wedding trip at all—the groom's headed over there.

"What do you hear?" I ask Greg, who spent the day at Fort Dix. "Nothing yet," he says.

"Nothing" sounds good, I think. *Let's keep it that way.*

Over the decades since Vietnam, many more of us have come to see that it is possible to differ on whether to go to war without demonizing one another. We do this better at some times than at others, but for the most part, I do not observe the widespread scorn with which the antiwar movement in those days viewed the actual young people who waged that war. And, more now than I ever did then, I hear those who support the war able to understand those who do not. At the very least, they know what can happen if they cannot listen.

Cool music and tie-dyed shirts aside, the sixties were a terrible time. America was rent asunder by the war. We were cruel to each other, buying the adrenaline of good feelings about our own fellow travelers with the coin of contempt for those with whom we disagreed. I do not want to live like that again.

Perhaps, this time around, prayer will change us. It can do that if we will let it. If prayer is the lining up of our own hearts and wills with the mighty stream of God's will, so that we and those for whom we pray are together carried forward into the future by that mighty river, we can widen our prayers beyond the boundaries of our desires and opinions. We can pray without fear for those we love. We can pray for our enemies without disloyalty. We can peer into dense fog of the unknowable future and consign it to the care of a loving God, in whose hand history rests.

We can pray for peace. We can pray for those in harm's way. We can pray for all the leaders of the nations—they all need it. We can pray for the people of all the nations—they need it even more. We can pray for the safety of the innocent. We can pray for an end to hostility. We can pray for wisdom and discernment.

What will happen in the world when we pray like that? It is in the nature of history that we cannot know what will happen in the world. We never know. But something will happen. It happens in the one who prays, and it happens in the world as well. Prayer changes us.

Most gracious God, look upon the world you have made with the same love from which you formed it. Stamp upon every heart the knowledge that all human beings in every place are made in your image, and that we can never renounce our membership in the human family. Present and preserve peaceful means of resolving the strife of nations, and give to all leaders the courage and grace to lead toward a good that is wider than their own immediate interests. Bless those who do not plan wars but must wage them, and bless those caught in their crossfire. These things we ask in the Name of Jesus Christ, the Prince of Peace, who lives with you and the Holy Spirit, one God, maker and lover of one world. Amen.

The Alpha and the Omega

Early, early in the morning, a fleet of cats precedes me down the stairs to the kitchen. We find the motion of trotting cats amusing: their backs remain perfectly still, their legs scissoring rapidly back and forth as they progress. I am very slow descending stairs, so they are already lounging around the kitchen when I appear, each of our two visiting cats holding back uncertainly.

This is because, like us, cats in groups seek to establish a hierarchy of power and privilege. They can't just live together as equals: somebody has to be the alpha, and everyone else has to know it. The alpha eats first. The alpha chooses where to sleep first. The alpha protects his—or her—position with aggressive behavior. When they are resting together in the same spot, the other cats in the group arrange themselves with respect to the alpha—the alpha occupies the highest spot, and the others face him. Or her.

Simba is the largest. And he is the only male. Oughtn't he be the alpha? Those two facts seem to count for little here, though: he displays great timidity at breakfast time. He does not join the others in their group harangue while I'm filling the bowls. He does not leap up onto the counter as Gypsy does, hoping to be first. He hangs back until everyone else has begun, only tentatively approaching the bowl I put out for him, once he has begun to eat, and fleeing it altogether if I even walk by.

Q says this is not timidity at all. It is kingliness, he says. Simba is an enlightened monarch, concerned with his subjects' needs. That is why he waits for the girls to eat. I set his bowl out in the hallway. Maybe the king wants a private dining room. But when I walk by, he runs away. *Uneasy lies the head that wears a crown.*

Oh, please. I don't think Simba is a king at all. At best, he is a cowardly lion.

I enter the living room in the afternoon. Little Gypsy, the youngest of all the cats, is curled on the couch in a sunny spot. Simba is on the floor, stretched out near the heat. Kate is sleeping in her chair. What's-Her-Name is sitting on the floor, gazing at Q, who is reading in his chair. Of all the fauna in the living room, Q is in the highest spot.

So a decision has been reached. Q is the alpha cat.

The dog sleeps on a corner of the couch, oblivious to all the power arrangements. She seems uninterested in power: Dancer is all about love. Dogs have trained us well, I read in an article recently: all they have to do is gaze into our eyes and lick our hands, and we'll feed them for the rest of their lives. It says in the article that they don't really love *us,* that all this adoration is just adaptive behavior designed to make us love *them.* And feed them.

Well, it works. We'd do anything for Dancer. But then, we'd do anything for the cats, too, and they don't gaze adoringly into our eyes. We love them. We don't really know, I guess, what animal love is like, or even if there's such a thing.

But we do know our own love. Human love at its best inverts power. It serves when it could rule. It transforms menial attentions—feeding, grooming, changing diapers, chauffeuring—into sublime man-ifestations of love. We knew about that before Christ came among us—we had learned it in just this way, from our pets, our parents, from our children, from all of our loves. And now our life in Christ lifts up such servant love to us and locates it right in the center of heaven: God *is* that kind of love.

We need look no further.

The Cost of Growing Stronger

"Who is that?" Q wants to know.

"I'm not sure," I say, pointing with my toe at a bright green, rather bulbous shoot just breaking the soil out front. I have dragged him out here to see the first brave little explorer of the spring. It's where I put some of the 100 daffodil bulbs I stooped over last fall, but it doesn't look like a daffodil. It looks like a tulip. This is unlikely. The first little explorer is usually a snowdrop or a crocus, and usually has some company. This guy's alone. Maybe I put something in there that I've forgotten; squirrels do that, I read. They forget one out of every four nuts they bury. That's why we have trees.

We'll just have to wait and see.

Prune your butterfly bushes almost down to the ground in the spring, it says in one of the garden books. The flowers come on the new growth. Such severe pruning is a frightening thing to do: there you stand, your shears in hand, coldly clipping feet of growth off a living thing. Without administering an anesthetic. Will it work? Have I just turned a wonderful four-foot bush with lovely sweeps of purple blooms into a bunch of twelve-inch spikes for the year?

Houseplants are the same. They need to focus their energy, so you prune them: cut terminal buds, inches of growth, cut it right off. Makes them bloom. You've done it before, and it works. Each time, though, it's frightening. You mean I have to lose what I'm holding right here in my hand for the sake of something I don't see yet? I walk by a geranium and snap off an inch or two of stem, just above a leaf node. Take that.

You mean I have to lose what I have in order to grasp what I want? Sometimes you do. It's a cold decision you make, when you do that— we want to keep what we have, hate losing it, even hate losing it if it's a source of frustration and sorrow. *At least it's mine,* we think to ourselves, and we cling to the spindly, unproductive stems of it long after they're doing us any good.

What would you be if you dropped the thing you're holding onto simply because you've always held onto it and for no other reason? If you stopped doing something you do only because you've always done it and didn't have the courage to stop? Something that carries no strength or joy for you, just the burden of history and nothing more? Something that sucks power from you for the things that uniquely constitute your call.

Scared, is what you'd be. Incredulous at your own audacity. Uncertain, and acquainted with something like dread. But at the moment of the pruning, when the shears bite through the stem, when you finally set down the load, step out into a new light, raise your eyes from your next predictable footstep to a horizon of which you have dreamed but never thought you'd ever see, you will know a new power. God promises life. Accepting the promise takes guts.

Things Cats Do

"You could write about what the cat did to my new sweater," Q said. I was soliciting eMo ideas from him, as I often do. I used to pester Bobby Hecht for them when we worked together at St. Clement's. Bobby could always come up with something.

Actually, it's much easier than you'd think to have a fresh idea for an eMo every day. Everybody has fresh ideas all day, every day. All you have to do is choose one of them and write about it. Give it its head—do we know what that means anymore, now that we drive cars instead of horses? It means you just hold the reins loosely for a spell, and let your horse go where he wants to go. You let your idea remind you of things.

As I begin, an Instant Message from Cynthia in Texas appears on the screen. Her cat died yesterday at fourteen. As God's special cat providence so frequently arranges, a kitten had broken into her house just two weeks before through a tear in the window screen. "I warned you about that neighborhood ...," I wrote. In any event, the Lord giveth and the Lord taketh away. The new kitten's name is Burglar.

Cats will break into your house more often than you might think. There are sophisticated rings of cat burglars—actual cats, not the human kind—in most American towns. Our neighbor's cat broke into the house two doors down from them, and ended up arrested. They saw his mug shot on television, and had to go down to the pound to bail him out. This was years ago, and I'm sorry to say that Banana is completely unrehabilitated. He breaks into our place all the time.

Which brings us to the sweater. It is a wonderful Irish-from-Ireland fisherman's sweater, a gift from our friend Barbara. It replaces Q's old one, which he wore into a gossamer torso-shaped web of holes.

It is heavy and warm, just like the old one. He adores it.

Was it Banana? Did he break in and pee on Q's new sweater? I wouldn't put it past him. Or was it one of the "girls," made nervous by Banana's presence on the periphery of the house—they often express their displeasure at his lurking in this most unpleasant way. Or could it have been mild Simba, announcing that he—not Q—really is the alpha cat, even if he's a big wimp?

The Irish sweater is heavy. Soaked in water and soap, it's even heavier: it weighed ten pounds, I'm sure. I washed it in the bathtub to avoid stretching and wringing, filling and draining through a dozen cold rinses, until the water ran clear. I rolled it in a heavy towel so it would dry more quickly, and it still took two entire days. But it smells sweet again; no trace of cat anywhere. Ready for the next insult.

For there will be a fresh insult. There always is. Cats and kids. Jobs. Churches. Lovers. There is always something, some new hurdle to surmount, some new broken thing to fix, some new problem to solve. Things never stay *just so*. You know you're alive when you have problems. The only people who don't have them are the dead.

One cat dies. Another pees on your best sweater. Another breaks into your house. One problem is contained, and another one bursts into flame. The one you love is certain to be the thorn in your side, at least part of the time. We are magnificently in the image of God, we who arise each morning into only one certainty: that there will be problems today we haven't anticipated, and that we will have to think and move fast in order to stay ahead of them.

Praise God for the thinking. Praise God for the moving. Praise God that we are not yet lying still. That will come soon enough.

The Heresy of Loneliness

Another unpreparedness dream: I was late to the service at Trinity, not vested, not ready. I grabbed a red cope that I saw hanging all alone on a coat rack—a big clue that this was just a dream—as I ran into the sacristy. They were just lining up. But my red cope didn't match: everyone else was in white.

There was no verger to be seen—another big clue—and so I just got in line, a scarlet gash in the neat line of white, and we began to move out. As we walked down the center aisle, I debated: would it be better to lose the red cope and be there in my white surplice? Or just tough it out in the wrong color? What to do?

Unpreparedness dreams are heretical. They are fearful visions of what life would be like if we had no help. In dreams of unpreparedness, we have failed to do what we needed to do, and the jig is finally up. But we are also all alone in those dreams: we burst into the room, run along the deserted hallway, enter the classroom where the exam is already in progress, everyone else studiously bent over her bluebook while we are stammering out excuses at the door. All alone.

There is the heresy. We're not alone. Nobody is going to be in the liturgy at Trinity in the wrong cope—the vergers will make sure it's the right one. You can be dumb as dirt, but it won't show in the liturgy. People take care of you. You don't have to do it all yourself. Until it's time to preach the sermon, of course. Then you really *are* on your own.

Or are you? The Holy Spirit is available to us. It never leaves us. The Spirit waits patiently for us to understand our need, and stands ready to supply it. Dreams of unpreparedness show forth our great fear, the fear of our own inadequacy and the fear of our aloneness in the face of it. But the Spirit is adequate beyond our limits. And makes our limits larger than we think they are.

The Holy Spirit adds the element of love to each daunting task you face. Your effort is not just for you: it's for the world. Even the loneliest artist's work is a work of communication, and the striving of those of us who are not solitary in our work, all the more so: we're here for each other. My sermon is not for me; it's for the congregation. God doesn't bring people out on a Sunday morning so they won't grow. We can trust that God's purpose for us includes those whose lives we touch. We'll be given the grace to go beyond ourselves if we need it, and if we will accept it.

Every time I have an unpreparedness dream, I ask to be delivered from the loneliness of my heresy. For the grace to ask for help. For the grace to rise above my self-absorption and see my work as service. If I can do that—remove the neurotic focus from my own drama, and put it instead on the ones whom I serve—the task will be okay. Because my work is not really about me. It's about them.

A Box of Hummingbirds

This year, a new approach: I will not pursue the hummingbirds quite so desperately. I will not hang red balloons in the trees. I will not get up before dawn every other day to change the sugar water. I will not color the sugar water red.

This came to me amid the snowdrifts of Buffalo, where hummingbirds are but a faint summer memory. Susan was driving. Genevra was in the back seat. Instead of the usual travel occupations of counting oncoming cars or contemplating the eternal question—"Are we there yet?"—we were talking about gardens and garden animals. Susan wondered if anybody sells hummingbirds, the way they sell ladybugs to come to your house in a jar and eat the aphids off your plants. Many of the ladybugs just fly away as soon as you let them out. Sometimes not a single one stays. They're in it for themselves, basically. There's no way to predict them.

None of us had ever heard of any professional hummingbirds coming to your house in jars. All the hummingbirds in Western New York are volunteers. All hummingbirds everywhere are volunteers. Selling someone a bunch of hummingbirds would be like giving him a box of air: gone the moment you open it.

A great weight fell from me, the weight of all my futile eagerness to please them. I should already have learned this from the cats, but it only came to me now: you can't make animals come to you. Be as attractive as you can, and have on hand what they might like if they do come, but don't count on it. They're volunteers.

Mostly all you have to do is love them. Love their being in the world. Glory in their beauty, no matter where they are. Marvel over their photographs, their colors. But do not need them. They can't really be

---

164

here for you. They are here for themselves.

Each of us is here on earth with a unique de
be owned, and none of us can be controlled, not co
ever. We must learn to be all right on our own. W
matters, a life bountiful enough to overflow a bit i
ers for their good. Nobody who goes looking for h
happiness exists only as a byproduct of a life well lived.

February 2 is the Feast of the Presentation, a chance for us to glimpse a rite of passage in an ancient childhood: you take your baby to the temple and present him to the priest, and you offer a sacrifice of thanksgiving for his birth.

Or that's how *we* would word it on the invitations.

Actually, the custom really wasn't about giving thanks for the baby at all. It was about purifying the mother from the ritual uncleanness brought upon her by childbirth. Girls made you more unclean than boys, it seems—the mother had to wait thirty-three days to be purified after a boy's birth, as against the sixty-six she waited after having birthed a girl. Then she brought the animal she could afford—lambs for the rich, pigeons for the poor—to the door of the Tent of Meeting, where the priest met her and gingerly received the animal, without touching the dirty mother. When he had ritually killed the animal, sprinkled its blood on the altar in the proper way and burned the meat, she was clean. Hundreds of animals, every day. Should time travel ever become possible and you get the chance to visit ancient Israel, don't sign up for Altar Guild in the Temple, no matter what they tell you.

Many of us remember the Churching of Women from the 1928 prayer book, where it was euphemized as "The Thanksgiving of Women after Child-Birth." And it *was* a thanksgiving. But fragments of fear survived in it: a warning that the mother be "decently appareled," a suggestion that the rite be done in "some convenient place"—earlier books put her safely outside the choir door—a requirement that she bring an offering to be put to use in relief of other women in childbirth. I remember my mother and her friends, in their hats and gloves, their dark blue suits, their tweed skirts. It never would have occurred to them to come to church other than "decently appareled." You wore a lace doily on your head, if you didn't have a hat, and you kept it in your purse in a little pouch, just in case. But you didn't come into the church bareheaded.

The practice carries hints, also, of something much more fearsome: the sacrifice of animals was probably a mitigation of an earlier practice, one that was long lost by the time of Jesus. We see traces of it in the pages of the Old Testament, where prophets inveigh against it: the sacrifice of the newborn child itself. The ritual mutilation of circumcision, the sacrifice of a pigeon—better than the killing of a child. The Hebrew Scriptures distance their own community from it, telling us that child sacrifice was a practice of the barbaric neighbors of the Israelites. But why, then, did the people of Israel themselves have to be warned against sacrificing their own children? Warned repeatedly? We read the story of Abraham and Isaac, and wonder why Abraham went along with the terrible idea of sacrificing his own son so meekly. It was because it wasn't the first he'd heard of it. In ancient, ancient times, the forebears of our faith probably did it, too.

Candlemas, we also called the Feast of the Presentation. People used to bless and light candles, and walk in procession with them, singing the Song of Simeon, the old priest who recognized Jesus as the Messiah when his mother came to fulfill the ancient rite of purification. "I can go in peace now," says the old man's song, "because I have seen the Savior." The Candlemas procession was beautiful. It is still done in some places. Beautiful. Nothing scary about candles.

The history of the church is like your baby photographs, like your yearbook from the 1960s—*I wore that?* you say as you quickly turn the page. Yep, you wore it. Yep, we did those things, and believed those things. And then we grew up. We're growing still.

We don't dismiss our faith because we know scary things about its origins. No phenomenon is understood simply by understanding its beginnings. History goes on. We go on. "Jesus grew in wisdom and stature," it says in the Gospel reading, "and in favor with God and mortal alike." Our story isn't finished until it's finished, and we don't do ourselves any good by trying to put a good spin on our past. Or by running away from it.

The Gospel reading for the Feast of the Presentation, which includes the Song of Simeon, is Luke 2:22–40.

The Hope of Us

Gypsy stands at the kitchen window all morning, in an activity Q refers to as "watching TV." We have a bird feeder attached to the window with a one-way mirror as its backing, so that you can see the birds who come to it, but they can't see you.

This is Gypsy's dream come true—birds who go quietly about their business, unaware of her presence inches away. Her muscles tremble slightly, and her tail twitches with the thrill of the chase. Once in a while, she swipes at the window, and the dream crumbles: she will never reach the birds at the feeder. They will always be behind the glass. So near, and yet so far.

You would think she'd give up, but she never does. She watches and waits, looks at the birds and longs for them, and once in a while, even though she knows it's crazy, she reaches for them.

Actors are like that. Writers, too. All artists are, in fact. Successes in art are much rarer than failures. You audition a lot more often than you get the part. You submit much more than you publish, at least at first. Hardly anybody makes money: if money is your only reward, an arts career is not for you.

But the failures in the artist's life aren't really failures: they're just early incarnations that died pointing to another approach that might be better. Every artistic failure is a martyr to the cause of excellence. A painter uses and reuses a canvas, scraping off a failed attempt and beginning again. And again. Museum technicians can look beneath the surface of an old painting to the even older attempts beneath, layer upon layer, sometimes.

We are so hopeful. We sit down at the computer, stand at the easel, get out the cake pans, pick up the calculator, thread the needle, overturn the first spadeful of earth, all in such hope. God will look down on us and see us creating, and God will remember the making of the earth, its many oddities, those created things whose purpose is hidden from us, those created things we may think would have been better off left on the drawing board. God made them anyhow.

"WHY, MY SIX-YEAR-OLD COULD DO A BETTER JOB THAN THAT!" someone says loudly in a museum. *Then your six-year-old knows the purpose of art better than you do, ma'am,* I say silently. It is about reaching, about trying, about tinkering until it seems just right, and then about the risky business of sharing what you have made with somebody besides your mother. It is about loving the experience of creating itself, loving the smell and feel of it, loving the hours that stretch out while doing it, loving the hopeful humming of *making* that you feel in your very body.

Maybe we are art to God. If so, if the universe is God's creation, God must be very happy. The hopeful music of the creation must be very beautiful within the mind of God. God must hum, still, with the making of us.

The Way We Were

In the background of answering my email, the television is on—it is in my office. It is a program about mummies in Egypt, beginning with King Tut, of course, and going forward in time to the latest mummies, from a time when the rites of embalming were available to anyone with the money to pay for it—not just royalty. Interesting: ancient Egyptian society had a progression like ours, in which more and more people got money, and with it the desire for the finer things of life. In their society, one of the finer things was getting your brain and other innards removed and pickled in a jar after you died, while they wrapped the rest of you in strips of linen and left you to dry in the sand so that people thousands of years hence could wonder about you.

The program said that the priests in ancient Egypt were the ones who did this. Hmmn. Seminary must have been a very different experience in those days.

It also said that you could get your cat mummified with you, or someone else's cat, or a cat especially raised for the purpose of someday becoming a cat mummy. One of their gods—Bastet (or Pasht or Ubasti), the one with a cat's head—wanted her fellow cats killed and offered as mummies.

The cats were dispatched by having their heads twisted and their necks broken. You simply could not do this with What's-Her-Name. It wouldn't be worth it. She'd tear you to ribbons. In fact, I can't imagine any cat going quietly. It's as much as your life is worth just to try to give them a pill. Perhaps the cats of Egypt belonged to a gentler age.

It mattered so much to those long-ago people that all the parts be there, that the bodies of the dead be put back together in another place, that they have all the things they needed—furniture, food, dishes, even their own slaughtered servants, who would rise again to resume their lives of drudgery on the other side.

We wonder what life is like there. What survives? We long for it to be everything, to go on as we were here, only forever. We want the beloved dead to look the same, to act the same. We want to know them as we knew them.

Most of all, we want them to love us. We want them to remember. The idea that they are changed makes us sad. Changed? We liked them the way they were.

Of course, nothing is just the way it was. Not even here. Every moment is unique, and will never come again. We do not go backward in time here. Each moment is over as soon as it is born.

And they do not have time there. Nothing is lost there. Everything is in the present for them—the main difference between their lives and ours is that we lose everything and they lose nothing. We cling to the stuff of life—to our looks, to our youth, then to the fiction of our youth, terrified of losing what we have—all because we can't grasp that all that is good still will be retained in the kingdom of heaven.

And why would we grasp it? We're mortal, with the nearsightedness that mortality always entails. All we know is here, and most of us love it so much here that we don't ever want to leave. Some of us are terrified even thinking about it.

But we don't have to be afraid. A life of prayer prepares us to live in peace, but it also prepares us to leave in peace. A prayer in the Daily Office for Friday evenings talks about going to sleep in Christ and waking in his likeness. It chooses the peace of nighttime sleep as a model for the repose of the dead, and suggests that this longer sleep is a beginning, not an ending.

Perhaps you are reading this in the morning. Perhaps you know something of what is ahead today. Perhaps you dread part of it. All of it. But you cannot know everything. Nothing is what it was. This morning, everything is new. May God bless it to your use.

Idol Meat

One of my first seminary papers was written on the subject of idol meat. St. Paul devoted a large part of his first—it wasn't really his first, by the way—letter to the Corinthians to idol meat. I loved the macabre sound of it. Idol meat. Hee hee.

So, of course, I was thrilled to see that we'll be hearing about idol meat in church this Sunday. Oh, happy day.

What's an idol? I asked the fourth- and fifth-graders last week. We were creeping through the Ten Commandments, and were just about to leave the second one behind with a quick wrap-up before we get down to the real business of taking the Lord's Name in vain. "It's a rock star," one of them told me, "like in *American Idol*," and I began to remind them about idol worship and carved wooden gods and temples. Language changes, though. To them, an idol is a rock star first. To them, its historical meaning will always be a secondary definition. Sort of like Madonna. "It also means the Blessed Mother of Our Lord," I tell them. "Really? Cool!" they say, "Jesus' mom was named after Madonna!"

And what is idol meat? What does that sound like to them? Cannibalized rock stars, I suppose. Rock Star *en brochette*. Rock Star *au gratin. Tournedos de* Rock Star.

They offered meat to their gods, the ancient people, just as the Jews offered meat to our God in the temple at Jerusalem. Cut it up on the altar and burned some of it. Gave some of it to the priests. Ate the rest. So they would ingest holiness.

We are not far from them, really. We ingest holiness in the Eucharist—it is not actual meat, but it is the real presence of Christ, the Body and the Blood. We are sanctified by its reception. That's what pagans thought about their ritual consumption of meat sacrificed to their

---

gods, too, and new Christians were afraid: *What if I go to somebody's house and eat meat that has come from an idol's temple by mistake?* they worried. *I'll be tainted by it. The idol will be inside me, take me over.* Other, more sophisticated Christians scoffed at the concern. Don't be silly. An idol is nothing.

But Paul was wiser. Yes, an idol is nothing. But just because *you* know that doesn't mean *everybody* does. An idol is nothing. But that doesn't mean you can't spend energy and sow confusion in your own soul and the souls of others by hanging around with one. An idol encourages me to place something created above the Creator, and to venerate it far beyond its worth. I am apt to invest it with honor beyond what it deserves. I am apt to make it my God. It won't be able to sustain the weight of my devotion, and, eventually, I'll be left godless.

Sophistication isn't always the friend of faith. You can talk yourself into anything if you're smart enough and good with words. An idol can never hurt us. It has no real existence. But our idolatry does exist. It's very real. And it can take us far from where we long to be.

The Epistle for the Fifth Sunday after Epiphany, Year B, is 1 Corinthians 9:16–23.

Love and Work

"I did plant those wildflowers," Q said. He had been catching up on his eMos, and had gotten to one about how it was time to plant the wildflower seeds I had bought ages ago and how the latest dump of snow—one of several successive snows which had prevented it—was making me itchy.

"Where did you put them?"

"In Dancer's Hole."

"Dancer's Hole" sounds like a small town in the American West. It isn't, though: it's the largish cavity Dancer the Dog dug at the base of a tree over the seven weeks she was visiting us. Dancer's Hole was quite a project: she would dash around and around in happy, low-to-the-ground circles, stop abruptly at the tree and dig furiously, tear around again, as many rotations of dashing and digging as she could accomplish until we called it all off and made her come back inside.

She was so resolute about digging her hole. And so happy about it. We knew we'd have to plant something in it to remember her visit. So Dancer's Hole will sprout wildflowers. That'll be nice.

Dancer's Hole was her work, I guess. Love and work, Freud said: that's what human beings need. Maybe even dogs need love and work: they're famous for their loving ways, but her approach to the hole was workmanlike indeed. Workmanlike, but joyful.

Her attitude toward her work was as joyful as her attitude toward love. We envy dogs their unqualified joy—it eludes us. It seems to us, so often, that we fall passively into our work, that somehow it happens to us, that we suddenly find ourselves there with no clear idea of how we came, that we squander forty and more hours weekly on something we don't care much about. I need the money, we say to ourselves, and that's the truth. Work beats starving any day.

But Freud thought it was as important as love. He thought we needed both in our lives to be complete. I've always thought so, too, and have regarded the unboundaried hours of the unemployed as an ongoing sorrow as great as their loss of income. It doesn't feel like as great a sorrow at first—*Well, at least I can sleep later in the morning*—but it is every bit as profound. We take so much of our shape from the rhythm of our work. So much of our sense of self.

I've always derived way too much of my sense of self that way. *You can't earn your way into heaven,* I would read, and I would nod. Yes, of course. I knew that. *God's love is unconditional,* someone would tell me, and again I would nod. This is true. But I had no emotional connection with what it might be like to think I was loved no matter what I did. Everyone else was loved unconditionally, but somehow I was not.

How foolish it is. To think that something applies to everyone but me. To think that I'm so exceptional. To think that I alone must run myself ragged until the joy is sucked out of all my good work.

Heresy. We don't work to win God's love. God just loves us. We work to be like God, in our small way, to create as God creates, to serve as God loves, to bring God's ways more and more into fleshly existence in history. We even work, as Freud thought we did, to be more and more our very selves.

We work the way the wildflower seeds work. Their bloom is self-initiated, and their bloom is what they are for. It is their work. Flowers are what they make. It is in their nature, and it is in ours. Their beauty is their way of expressing love and joy in the work they do. So our work can be beautiful, too, whatever we do for a living. Freud must not have gone far enough. It's not just love and work we need. We need love *in* work as well.

Duct Tape

Eleven directees, one right after another: Tuesday was a busy day. They arrived by subway, by railway, by car, on foot.

Penn Station bristled with police officers and soldiers. Ditto the Port Authority. An enormous police van blocked the southwest entrance to Central Park. Hotels and department stores, someone on the radio said, are especially vulnerable. The organizers of Sunday's peace march still don't have the permit they want. The city might as well issue it: hundreds of thousands will come, permit or no. An NYPD nightmare.

And I also hear on the radio that we're all supposed to lay in a supply of plastic sheeting and duct tape.

Duct tape! Thank God. We have duct tape. A nice fat roll of the magical stuff lives permanently in our pantry, right next to the birdseed, where we'll always be able to lay our hands on it. Is there anything a human being cannot do with duct tape? Any tear that cannot be mended, leak temporarily fixed, any split tool handle that cannot be made whole? Is there a treacherously frayed electrical cord that cannot be swaddled into harmlessness with the silvery bands, a tempting outlet that cannot be shielded from curious toddler fingers with duct tape?

Perhaps I will purchase another roll, today, and carry it in my purse from now on. A prepared citizenry is the best line of our defense. I will perform a citizen's arrest of terrorists outside Macy's, and bind their hands behind their backs with my duct tape. Then I will stabilize the famous windows with a silver cross on each one. I will gag politicians with duct tape—maybe I should get two rolls. I will sheath my torso with a breastplate of duct tape, protecting my inner organs from any blow and keeping them all together for ease of sorting later on.

Duct tape?

Perhaps this instruction is not as surreal as it appeared to me when I heard it, but it prompted inappropriate laughter in me, laughter far in excess of the joke. Nervous laughter, I guess. I listened to myself laugh, and decided to be alert to fear among my directees.

Some I asked. Some volunteered. Yes, they were afraid. Frustrated at their powerlessness. Fearful for their children, and for themselves. We talked of setting meeting places in advance for family members to gather if they become separated. We talked of obligation to stay in the city and help in an emergency versus obligation to get home. Obligation to try and stay alive.

And we talked of heaven, and of those who might die if we are attacked again. Everyone won't die. Some will, and some won't. There is no way to tell in advance. Where? When? Who? We cannot know.

But we do affirm that this life, for which we now fear, is not the only life there is. It is ephemeral, but it sits in the larger basket of the life beyond it, utterly mysterious to us, unknowable. Unknowable but good.

We think of that life as another home. A better one. We imagine it as being like home, complete with our deceased relatives who come out to meet us, who recognize us and love us still, who look like they did when we were together. We know nothing, and so we make things up.

That's all right. We are better off, even now, if we allow ourselves to believe. Such faith can never be proved right or wrong: it is not the stuff of proof. We should walk carefully in making confident assertions about its architecture or membership requirements, but we should fling ourselves with abandon on its mercies. We need them. Nothing is to be gained by holding ourselves back from faith. Nothing but fear.

Be Over-prepared

That was stupid, going outside in a blizzard with a tin of birdseed for the feeder, wearing only a bathrobe and slippers. I would only be a second, I thought as I opened the door and slipped out. I do it all the time. And it did only take a second to feed the birds. But the snow is a foot deep. It took less than a second for it to fill the space between my bare feet and the shearling lining of the slippers. Ugh. Now the slippers are upside down over the heating vent.

I love the way this part of the world paralyzes itself over a snowstorm. In Minnesota, they don't. You have to be game out there. You have to get everywhere. Schools never close—once in a blue moon. They couldn't: kids would never get an education if they did. And you're not really allowed to complain about it. You'd look foolish out there, griping about something as omnipresent as snow.

Happily, it is not so with us. We can treat a heavy snow as a state emergency: the governor of New Jersey did that this morning, along with governors of several other states. We can declare a snow sabbath, cancel things, accept the gift of an extra day that falls into our laps as if it's leap year. And, if we are what the radio calls "essential personnel," we can bask in the more rugged comfort of that status: we are essential. Brave. Well-nigh indispensable. Able to leap tall buildings in a single bound. We can stomp into the places that need us so desperately in our heavy boots, cheerful and strong, heedless of the weather. Essential.

Odd: snow or no, I know spring is coming. I can feel it. In a month, maybe sooner, the crocuses will be up. I have dog-eared the seed catalogue until at last I am ready, and today I will order too many seeds, which will annoy Q, a measured man who will never understand the value of having more than enough, just in case.

I overdo everything, and it troubles him. I serve him too much food, use too much soap, make too much tea. "Can't you just take what you need?" I suppose I could. But how would I know for sure, in advance, what that might be?

To me, overdoing everything is the imitation of Christ. The stuff of creation, spilling over the sides of whatever seeks to contain it and all over the floor. Way too much. There is never just the right amount of grace. It is not measured. It is not sensible. There is more than enough. It is free and abundant.

It is free and abundant because life is hard. Many things are born because many things die. Grace runs in a hard, strong current through human life because human life is uncertain: we never know when we're going to need an extra helping. We can never plan for our uncertain needs. But God does.

A female downy woodpecker appears at the feeder outside my office window. The birds have been ignoring this feeder for several months—it is on the northeast side of the house, and it's colder over here. They prefer the sunny southwest, where the other feeders are. Maybe I should just take it down until the weather warms up, I have thought more than once.

But if I had, the little lady woodpecker who happened by in a blizzard wouldn't have found it. I predict that she will stick close to the tree all day, hopping on and off the feeder, out of the worst of the wind.

You never know when the foolish things you do will have a purpose that mirrors the divine grace. You wouldn't want to miss that.

God Is Yes

People in Jesus' time thought that illness arose from peoples' sins. They thought this happened in a fairly immediate cause-and-effect relationship. They had thought so for a long time—many of the psalms, like Psalm 41, allude to the idea: "Heal me, for I have sinned against you."

Today we are more apt to think that illness afflicts us in a more random way. He "caught" a cold, we say, or he "developed" a tumor. Jesus, in the story of his healing of the paralytic, seems to offer his hearers room for both approaches: "Your sins are forgiven," he tells the stricken man, and a collective murmur of shock and disbelief goes up from the crowd at his presumption in declaring forgiveness of sins: *Who does this guy think he is?* To clear things up, then, he commands the paralytic to take up his bed and walk. The man gets up, picks up his pallet, and goes on home. Whether his malady arose from sin or serendipity, then, the man is healed.

"See," says God to Isaiah, "I am doing a new thing." You thought you knew how the world works, but you know only so much. There are surprises in store for all of you, so stay tuned.

Many diseases have been tamed—diseases which roamed the earth in ancient times, devastating all who crossed their paths. We have conquered so many that it seems to us that we must be able to conquer all of them. Perhaps now we will have a world without illness, we think to ourselves ... until something new comes along to terrify us. And even when it does, we have confidence in ourselves: a cure is possible for anything, we're sure, if we just put enough research and enough money into finding it. And so we walk and bike and run for The Cure. We give to the Cancer Society, and to the Heart Fund, and to the Diabetes Foundation. We no longer give up on the sick, no longer isolate them, content to believe that they have brought their illness upon themselves. That's ancient history.

Or is it? We *usually* don't give up on the sick. We *usually* don't think they brought it on themselves. Consider, though, the history of the AIDS epidemic, of the secrecy and shame in which it was veiled in this country for a full ten years before we faced it as a public health problem, of the euphemisms still employed in the newspaper obituaries of many who die of HIV-related illnesses. And consider the widespread devastation that same secrecy continues to cause in Africa, in Asia. For reasons of politics and public relations, government after government has refused to admit that AIDS was a problem in its country until it become almost insurmountable. The numbers are staggering: forty percent of the adult populations of some African nations may be infected. Half the children may become orphans in the next five years, with no healthy adults left to care for them at all. Denial has proved fatal. As it always does.

Or consider the history of mental illnesses. The New Testament assumed they were caused by demon possession. We don't think so today. Or don't we? We still cloak them in shame and secrecy. Gripping its victims in behavior that isolates them and frightens those around them, psychiatric illness is compounded when we treat it like a failure of nerve or a character flaw. People are ashamed to admit they have it, afraid someone will find out they're in therapy or that they take antidepressants. As if their illness were really a sin. And so they don't seek treatment, those who love them cannot understand their symptoms, and they suffer for decades. Research on cures for mental illness lags far behind that for other illnesses in urgency and funding. There are no telethons for schizophrenia, although 2.2 million adults in America are afflicted with it, as against the 250,000 who live with muscular dystrophy, another incurable disease, for which the Jerry Lewis Telethon alone raised $58,000,000 in 2001. Nobody wants to talk about mental illness.

And, if nobody talks about it, nobody can help.

Jesus couldn't have healed the paralytic if the man's friends hadn't been part of the project. He wouldn't have known about him. They had to work to get in to see Jesus: the door was blocked with onlookers, and they had to come in through the roof. We think of ourselves, of our caution, of our careful attitude toward our own longing for healing: we don't get our hopes up. What did they know that we don't know? What did they know that made them think this would work, that Jesus could do something new in this man's life? They must have been pretty sure, or they wouldn't have stuck their necks out like that.

Or pretty desperate.

Maybe. But I think it was this: they just loved their friend a lot. They hated what illness and pain were doing to him. Love was the force that propelled them forward into such extreme action. It made them brave—foolish, some of the onlookers might have said, but brave.

The Son of God is not "yes and no," St. Paul says. In him, it has always been "yes." We may not think God sends heart disease or cancer to people because of their sins anymore. We no longer charge God with the "no" in human history. But we do look to God for the "yes." We do know that God sends patient caregivers, dedicated researchers and physicians, devoted family and friends to walk with the ill through their painful journey, whether it be a journey toward cure or a journey toward the larger life. Such people are sent from God, whether they know it or not. Anyone who is part of the "yes" in any aspect of life—part of the healing, the comfort, the building up—is the servant of God.

More Heat

"Again?" I said to Q as Gypsy let out a guttural howl. "It can't be. She was just in heat a month ago."

But it was. Her distress deepened with the passing days, blossoming into a frenzy on exactly the day scheduled for the hoped-for surgery that will put an end to all this. No go.

"Can we reschedule as soon as possible?" I asked the vet. "Like two weeks?"

We'll see. Cats need to rest up a bit after their heat before anybody goes poking around at their insides. Last time we gave Gypsy a month to recover. Somehow, she must have known our intent, and the unmistakable howling began at twenty-seven days.

They go into heat more often if there are other cats around, the vet said. So that's it. There are definitely other cats around. She approaches them, sniffs them for possibilities, and turns away in despair at finding nothing.

Simba, of course, is a special case. He is a male cat, so that part is in place, but he's been neutered. We came upon them *in flagrante* yesterday—or, rather, we came upon them in the attempt at it. A puzzled Simba bestrode a writhing Gypsy, gripping her by the nape of her neck with his teeth. He looked up at us, his face more than usually blank. He was doing all the right things, but nothing was happening. *I used to know how to do this,* one could hear him thinking.

Q always feels sad about neutering the cats, depriving them of this pleasure in life. And it was sad to see, the two little animals trying to do what they were created to do, and finding some of the pieces missing. We assert with confidence that their attitude toward lovemaking is not like ours, that emotions are not involved, but who is to say? Their emotions may not be like ours, but their pain is obvious to anybody who sees it. This is not sufficient reason to litter the world with unwanted kittens, but it does give one pause. Their feelings may not be like ours. But we are not the only show in town.

This morning, Gypsy has been quiet so far. Perhaps the fever has passed. I hope so.

A Lonelier Day in the Neighborhood

Why was the radio announcer saying nice things about Mr. Rogers this morning? Why were they interviewing his colleagues? They just did that a few months ago, when he retired. Hoping against hope that it wasn't for the reason I feared it might be, I listened as the four cats circled me, watching closely while I spooned food into their dishes.

But it was. "Fred Rogers died yesterday," the announcer said, "at the age of seventy-four."

Oh, no. I paused, my spoon poised above one of the four feeding dishes, while reproachful cats circled me, scolding. Then I sighed and continued to spoon tuna into the bowls.

When my children had reached the end of their emotional ropes and nothing I did seemed to sweeten them up, he usually could. "Let's watch Rodge," I would say—Anna called him "Rodge"—and pretty soon there he would be, taking off his suit jacket and putting on his sweater, taking off his wingtips and putting on his sneakers, feeding his fish, listening respectfully while a guest fireman or cook or nurse or teacher talked. Gently—so gently that crankier humorists have parodied him for years—he would introduce topics likely to trouble a four-year-old: whether scary things on television are real, whether people who leave will come back, whether it's all right to get angry.

Often they didn't want to watch Mr. Rogers: "No!" they would howl in noisy despair. They didn't want to feel better. They wanted to stay distraught—odd, that: sometimes we would rather remain in our agitation than be guided out of it. But they must have known in their angry little hearts that watching Mr. Rogers would work, for they never offered more than token refusals. And soon two little girls would be sitting quietly, watching the toy train chug across the television screen into the Land of Make-Believe.

I had not known he was ill. I suppose his retirement not long ago had something to do with that, and that he preferred not to say so publicly. Always looking out for our feelings, Rodge, even at the end.

He was in my line of work. Ordained a Presbyterian minister, he spent most of his career being Mr. Rogers on the television. He didn't have a congregation in a church building. He didn't speak to his young audience about God, not directly, although he sometimes did to audiences of their parents and grandparents. But, if it is a pastor's work to lead people into reconciliation and truth, he was a fine pastor, church or no church.

Sometimes I wonder if my baby who died went on to grow in heaven? These and other absurdities crowd the minds of parents who have lost children. It doesn't matter much that we know heaven is not like earth—that doesn't stop us. We imagine it in the only terms we have available. I doubt that God minds much: it doesn't hurt God, and it comforts us. And so my silent little one is, for me, an eternal toddler, one of a throng of happy children in a bright and beautiful place, rather like a perfect nursery school. Healthy and at play in the sunny rooms, in the grassy playground, on the swings, shrieking and laughing.

Do we have jobs in heaven? If we do, I believe I know where Mr. Rogers works.

Armed, But Not Dangerous

"You keep your crosier in a gun case?" I asked as we approached the turnoff for the Atlanta Airport. A crosier is a staff shaped like a shepherd's crook that a diocesan bishop carries.

The bishop signaled for a left turn and eased off the highway. "Yup," he said, "the guy who made it insisted that I have a strong case that could accommodate the stand for it as well. He said he was sick and tired of the way bishops looked carrying their crosier stands around in a plastic Kroger's bag."

"Undignified," I agreed. But this was a fine time to bring it up: we were approaching the security checkpoint for the airport with what appeared to be a firearm in the car. What if we were stopped? It could be a long afternoon.

Apparently, they were profiling that day: the two large blond people sailed right through, gun case and all. We could have had a rocket launcher in the back for all they knew. They didn't even give us a glance when we came through the checkpoint a second time, in the course of our long search for a parking spot.

Like most liturgical equipment, the bishop's crosier is the fanciful descendant of a practical accessory: it started out as nothing more than a walking stick, something to help the bishop make it to the end of his totter down the aisle. Some centuries ago, somebody thought it would be nice if they were shaped like shepherds' crooks, the kind with a hook on one end, so you can gently lead the little lambs or, if gently leading doesn't work, give them a poke. A bishop takes crosier in hand and she reminds us of Jesus, we hope. The Good Shepherd.

Through Christ all things were made. Life comes from God through Christ, by the power of the Spirit. It draws us gently sometimes, and then sometimes it gives us a poke in the rear. We remember those times especially well. They sure don't feel like Jesus. But they may be. We can see it, sometimes, later on.

I'll Be Seeing You

Everything at the funeral was the way Joe wanted it. "I haven't picked the hymns yet," he said the last time I saw him, "but I will. Everything else is set."

He had ordered hospice care so he wouldn't have to go to the hospital. He didn't want to die there. He wanted to be at home. And he *was* at home. He hadn't been in hospice a week, hadn't even gotten to the point where he had round-the-clock nursing, before one day Grayce couldn't raise him on the telephone, and she and Steve let themselves into his apartment and found him sitting up in bed, the television still on.

My last pastoral call on Joe took place at a bar called Cleo's. People die as they live, Tolstoy said, and it is so: Joe was on his usual barstool, where he could look out the window and keep an eye on friends who passed by. He talked about how he was feeling, about the hospice people, about the funeral service. He was thin, now, and his hair was its natural white—he had colored it as long as I had known him, but I guess Joe had decided to die *au naturel*. His voice was weak, and he coughed a lot, but the bite of his wit was still in place.

"We're putting you next to Bobby's niche in the columbarium, so you guys can torment each other," I said. This always got a rise out of him.

"I'll come back and haunt the place if you do." It was an old joke. Bobby would always threaten to cut a tunnel between the two niches, so they could visit back and forth. "I'll make sure not to be home," Joe used to say, and everybody would laugh. St. Clement's was a place where you could joke about the columbarium and its citizens, and nobody thought it unseemly.

The funeral was in the theater, of course—St. Clement's has two worship spaces, one a beautiful new chapel, all sunshine and stained glass and clean, smooth wood, and the other a black-box theater, the oldest continuously used off-Broadway house in New York. Joe was a set builder—he built just about every show on Broadway in the 1960s, and used to make the rounds of the performances every night to make sure things were holding together before curtain time.

The congregation assembled, stopping to look at a wonderful picture of Joe at Grayce's birthday party—smiling, one arm raised in a greeting. *Come on in*, he seemed to be saying; *It's a party!* His daughter and her husband, his friends and fellow parishioners climbed the stairs and sat down in the theater seats. The lights dimmed. An onstage choir sat, unvested, along with the clergy and Bobby. It was an Episcopal service, straight from the prayer book, but the unusual setting showed forth the words in surprising relief.

Mitties de Champlain began with the ancient words that have comforted so many: "I am the resurrection and the life." We sang "O God, Our Help in Ages Past." The choir sang "May the Road Rise to Meet You." The theater seats thumped shut as people got up to receive communion, and at the end, we proceeded in silence to the chapel, where the columbarium is.

The light there was golden, like the light of heaven. The stone faces of the niches were smooth and clean, quiet like the spaces behind them. The congregation crowded in. We placed the urn into its resting place. Ashes to ashes. Dust to dust.

And from the last row of theater seats, looking down on the people of God, who thronged the chapel, a trio from the choir sang: "I'll be seeing you, in all the old familiar places...." And we dissolved in wondering smiles and hugs, a dance of love and remembrance, of tears and hope of heaven.

"He sang that song to me when I left New York," his daughter whispered, enfolded in her husband's arms, smiling and weeping at the same time.

Not a hymn, "I'll Be Seeing You." It's a standard of the American songbook, written by Irving Kahal with lyrics by Sammy Fain, a quiet farewell to a lost love. A song sung in some cabaret somewhere in New York every night since 1944, I'm sure.

Not a hymn, but it says what we know to be true: their lives are changed, but not ended. It's true. The dead are present with us in the communion of the saints, and they continue to participate in our world. It is we who cannot see them. They see us just fine. They love us still. They are in Christ now, as St. Paul says, and they are "all in all."

Go with God, Joe. I'll be looking at the moon, but I'll be seeing you.

Gifts Misused

Today is Gypsy's coming-out party, postponed twice now because of her raging hormones. She resented having to leave her comfortable chair, resented going into her carrying case, resented being at the vet's office. I imagine these complaints will fade into insignificance compared to what is about to happen to her, but it is for her own good.

I told the vet assistants about her disgraceful behavior. They nodded and laughed. I told them about our neutered male attempting to—well, *help* Gypsy through a difficult time, and how shocked we were. Then I asked a delicate question.

"Can a male cat—I mean, a neutered male, you know—can he ... can they, um, I mean, can they?..."

"They can't ejaculate," the young woman said simply, her eyes merry at my stammering.

"But, I mean, can they ... I mean, have, like ... sex?"

"Oh, yes. They can do it. They just can't sire kittens," she said. "Sometimes they do it to show dominance."

"Like some of their human counterparts, you mean?"

She laughed. "Yeah, like some of them."

So I guess the idea of castrating rapists, popular in some circles, wouldn't work as a preventive measure; if what they're doing is about dominance and rage, they don't need working plumbing to hurt people. They might even hurt them more, out of frustration. I was thinking along these grim lines because of a radio interview I was hearing about the movement to try children as adults. It is gaining strength throughout the country. The idea is that children who are accused of particularly heinous deeds should be tried in adult rather than juvenile court, as if it were the character of the crime that made one adult, rather than one's age.

toward Lent with sex and sin and death, crime and
mind. And war, of course. Sounds about right for
lay upon which all the fat things are greedily con-
pile excess upon excess, so that there will be noth-
om a more sober path.

We take the gifts of God and misuse them, turn the act of love into
a deed of hate, turn love of country into hatred of other countries, turn
desire for justice into thirst for vengeance. But in the forty days about
to begin, we have a chance to turn from our sins and live a different life.
We can choose. Alone among God's creatures here on earth, we can
evaluate ourselves and change our behavior. Alone among God's creatures, we can ask for help to change.

Poor Gypsy, in the grip of a sexual surge that was like madness.
No insight possible, not for her: just the rush of desire that made her
crazy. We love the cats, and anthropomorphize them whenever possible.
But we are not cats. We are not in the grip of our instincts and our hormones, our angers, not if we do not choose to be. Now is the time for us
to step back and make choices about how we will live in the world.

Cat in a Hat

Home from the vet, without so much as a thank-you for the $277 we dropped on her, Gypsy appears to be fine. And why should she thank me? She went in feeling perfectly well and came out eight hours later, woozy and sore and wearing a plastic funnel-shaped halo on her head so she can't bite at her stitches. It is secured with a bow under her chin, like a bonnet. She looks like a Jane Austen character. She must wear it for five more days. She hates it.

Q needs to work on his codependency issues around the cats. "I got her to eat from a spoon," he says. Gypsy had been having trouble getting down to her feeding dish with her bonnet on. He was afraid she wouldn't get anything to eat, and What's-Her-Name waited, ready to pounce on Gypsy's dish. But we've been down this road before: she will love eating her breakfast from a spoon held by her Q. Soon, she will refuse to eat any other way, even after the bonnet is off. Because he won't be able to bear the thought of her being hungry, he'll succumb. By the end of the month, she'll be getting breakfast in bed on a tray.

This is the way cats are. They want everything you can give them, and then they complain because you didn't give them more. And don't think she didn't notice the $277 just because she didn't say anything: she's keeping a ledger, and compares the dollars we spend on her with what we spend on the other cats. They all have accountants. Most of them insist on a few hundred a year, at the very least.

The bonnet feels to Gypsy as if she's gotten her head stuck in a hole. For a day, she kept walking backwards, trying to back out of it. But it didn't work. Now she's given up. Q tries to interest her in what we call her "television," a kitchen window with a bird feeder attached, the kind that has a one-way mirror, so you can see the birds but they can't see you. He fills the feeder from inside and closes the window. "Look, Gypsy!" he says hopefully when a bird comes. And, tail twitching with the thrill of the chase, she forgets the loathsome bonnet for a little while.

Distraction is a blessing. You can forget about a surprisingly high level of pain for a time, just by focusing on something else. You can learn not to pay so much attention to it.

Unlike the cats, human beings have the capacity to contemplate and think about their pains and their joys. We're pretty sold on the idea that our pain needs to be experienced and talked about, analyzed and shared, and that this is the way to make it better. Maybe. But sometimes we just need to find something else to do.

An All-Nighter in Eden

With a bumpy landing and only a little nausea—the people around me were concerned when I got out my airsickness bag, but it turned out to be a false alarm—I was back in Newark. "Has the snow melted yet?" I had asked Q on the phone the night before. I was calling from Dalton, Georgia, where daffodils are blooming and forsythias are thinking about it, where something called a "Lenten Rose," that we don't have in New York, already nods with her lavender cup-shaped flowers as you walk by her.

"It's just about gone," he had said, but there still seemed to be a lot of white in the patchwork of the ground as we wobbled toward the airport. Never mind: it's the 11th of March. The days must get warmer soon. The sun must shine longer. I have been away three days. That's a long time in a garden. There were bound to be some changes.

And yes, indeed: the crocuses are up, tiny spikes of them freckling the ground beneath the maple tree. More than last year: bulbs look quiet, but they have been thinking motherly thoughts under the ground all winter, and baby crocuses appear next to them in the spring. Some of the daffodils are up. The hollyhocks that I set out last September 11th made it through the winter—their leaves peek green from under their coverlet of mulch. I think Q's fig tree survived, swaddled as it was in pine branches.

I have longed to see these things. We have had a more appropriate blanket of snow this year than we have had in the suspiciously warm winters of the last several years. I have longed intensely for the sun, for green things, after months of grey skies and a white earth.

Plants survive winter because they are dormant in the cold. They sensibly lower the level of their activity to almost nothing and rest.

Hibernating animals do it, too: their heartbeats slow to less than half their normal rate, their breathing slows, they don't need to eat.

We don't do that. Winter is our busy season, our academic year, our selling season, our shopping season, our theater season. We bundle up and carry on, pack our office shoes in a bag and pull on our boots. We ignore our sleepy longing to stay in bed when it's cold.

Civilization demands it, I suppose. Look at what we've accomplished because we can work all night and run around all winter. Look where I can go because I can fly, and look at what I can do.

But there is something inside even us. Even we, who have conquered the effects of the seasons on our lives to so impressive an extent, remember that God placed us in a garden. We can't shake the longing for the new beginning spring will bring. We can't sleep the way the flowers sleep. But we can watch them awaken and thrill to it.

Freedom Fries

A late-ish hour and the fact that I had not eaten lunch did it for me: I didn't have to be asked twice if I wanted to go out to dinner. There is a new Indian place in Metuchen—local history, as it is our first Indian restaurant, even though many Metuchenites are from India, and two miles away in Iselin is a section so replete with gorgeous sari shops and restaurants that it's called Little India.

"We're so glad you're here," I said to the owner as he welcomed us. "We've needed you." The place was shiny and new. A floral arrangement from a well-wisher still stood on the counter.

The food was wonderful, and not just because I was so hungry. The complicated flavors followed one another and interwove, hot to sweet to hot to cool to savory, culminating in the lovely *amen* of steaming cups of Masala tea. The handles of the cutlery were shaped like twigs. The serving dishes were shiny copper. The teacups were painted with leaves of mulberry, the holy tree of India.

We always want to talk to the wait staff in Indian restaurants about India and how much we loved going there. About where they're from in India, and how long they've been here. About how often they get to go home for a visit. We're probably a nuisance, but they are always nice to us.

"That was absolutely wonderful," I said as we left. We walked past the Thai place, stopped at the drug store, and crossed the street at one of the coffee bars. In the car, we switched on the radio just in time to hear that the restaurant in the basement of the United States Capitol has changed the name of its French fries to "freedom fries."

How embarrassing. How utterly embarrassing to share a language with someone who would make up such a thing and think it witty. Some things are so stupid you just don't know where to begin.

"Wonder if we're going to send back the Statue of Liberty," Q asked as he started the engine. He informed me that this sort of thing is why Americans say "hot dog" instead of "frankfurter." An anti-German thing from World War I, he said. So how come we still have "hamburgers"? I suppose there's some comfort in the knowledge that this kind of lunacy isn't new. Or, let me think: maybe that's even more depressing.

Are we in for more of this? I hope not, but I fear so.

I wonder what God thinks about us. I've raised school-age children, and remember their ridiculous rivalries and how utterly frustrating they could be. How they won't sit on a chair because she sat on it and has cooties. How they argue over who's going to be in the front seat. How they abruptly drop a school chum because she is friends with someone else. This "freedom fries" business must look like that to God.

Eventually they grow up, though.

This is my prayer for the day:

That our current situation will fail to make us suspicious and insular; that it will not undo the fifty years of growth in ethnic and cultural diversity that have made America a better place than it used to be;

That we will not come to regard cruelty to others as a surefire sign that we love our country;

That we'll grow up, for heaven's sake.

For heaven's sake. Amen.

Sufficient Sacrifice

The Danish philosopher Søren Kierkegaard was fascinated by the story of Abraham's attempt to sacrifice his son Isaac. Kierkegaard ran a number of alternative scenarios in his mind of what might have transpired between the two during that walk up the mountain. What did they say to each other when Isaac was strapped down on the pile of firewood?

Think of it: *My dad and I are climbing the mountain with a load of firewood. When we get to the top, he ties me to the pile of wood and almost sets it on fire. He would have, too, if he hadn't noticed a sheep caught in the brambles nearby and sacrificed the sheep instead.*

Those who wish to explain this ancient story tell us that it's a story of how much Abraham loves God. How obedient he is to God. Okay. Kierkegaard isn't the only one who's had trouble with that.

But I have thought otherwise about this story. We know that the children of Israel were tempted to follow many of the religions they found among their neighbors in the ancient Near East. We know this because their prophets often warn them against joining in such worship: *don't go up and sacrifice in the high places* (Abraham and Isaac are heading up a mountain, aren't they?) and *don't pass your children through the fire* (Isaac bears a load of wood, doesn't he?).

Think of it. *Maybe the neighbors are right. Maybe we should be doing this, too.* Abraham is tempted to treat God as if God were Moloch, or some other deity who required the bloody sacrifice of one's own beloved child in fire. Abraham begins his terrible task. And God steps forth and stays his hand: *Stop. I am not Moloch. I am not this God of blood. I am not about murder. Here is a way for you to send me honor without offending against the holiest duty I have given you, the protection of your innocent child.* And Abraham sacrifices a sheep instead.

Today, we recoil, also, from the wholesale slaughter of animals that characterized temple worship among the Jews, even in Jesus' day, even slightly beyond. The temple was a bloody place, right up until the day in 70 A.D., when it was destroyed by the Romans. This destruction was the greatest tragedy any Jew could imagine at the time, but without it, we would not have the legacy of learning, logic, argument, and portable community that Judaism represents among us. We'd still have a people tied to Jerusalem, killing and burning animals in their temple.

Barbaric, we think to ourselves about such a thing. We think that we have become less and less bloody as we move through the centuries. In church that is true: no animal sacrifice anymore for us—although there can still be blood on the floor at certain vestry meetings.

Jesus, the Lamb of God, has been sacrificed for us, and it is enough. No more temple sacrifice. None needed. In the world, though, our hands are less clean. We kill more, not fewer, people than they did. Modern centuries are more bloody, not less so. We just do it more efficiently, and we arrange not to see or smell the blood.

From the cleanliness of our killing, from its smoothness and smartness, from the neatness of it, from its production values: Good Lord, deliver us.

This eMo was written in anticipation of the Second Sunday in Lent, Year B. The Old Testament reading about Abraham and Isaac may be found in Genesis 22:1–14.

My Worst Enemy

Nobody has been at the feeder outside my office window for ages—it's been too cold. They go to the one in back that gets more sun. But now the sun is getting over here earlier in the day, and Q reported a host of sparrows yesterday.

This morning, it was a female downy woodpecker. She was so still at first, I thought there was something wrong with her—she gazed into space as if hypnotized. "It's a feeder, ma'am," I said from my concealment inside. "You're supposed to eat." Finally another bird chirped from somewhere and shook her out of her reverie, and she began picking seeds out of the little holes.

Maybe she was cold. Or maybe the birdseed wasn't her brand—her kind really does prefer a nice suet block in cool weather. Or maybe she was just thinking. But she sat right there for a long time, with a wealth of what she needed right at her fingertips—well, wingtips—and did not reach out for it.

We know what that's like. It's good for me and I want it. I have the chance to reach for it and I ... just don't. For no good reason.

I'm not sure what it is that keeps me from doing what I really want to do when there is no obstacle to it except obstacles I make myself, but I do know that I'm not alone. "That which I would do, I do not, and what I would not do, that is what I do," is how St. Paul describes it, and I feel his frustration across the centuries.

"How did you do this week?" asked the doctor. We had had such an upbeat session last time. I was full of reasonable, concrete, and optimistic plans for eating and exercise. I would keep my food diary. I would wear my pedometer. I would do a lot of things.

I did some of them. For a while. A very short while. My virtue decayed quickly this past week, and I appeared at his office only reluctantly. "I'm so glad you could fit me in," I lied.

He was kind. This is another week. We made a few plans. We'll get together again a week from tomorrow. With God's help.

Le Jour de Gloire

It was Q's birthday. He wouldn't go with me to buy him a new trowel as a birthday gift—too busy fuming over Tuesday's class. And I know better than to buy him a trowel on my own—a person's trowel is an intimate object. So, since I had come home exhausted from my morning engagement, I slept the afternoon away instead.

I awoke to find he hadn't just been preparing for his class. He had been burning up the Internet notifying people about the 7 P.M. candle-light vigil in our town, one of more than 6,000 held throughout the country and even more in other parts of the world. He notified friends in other places about the vigil nearest them. Q's birthday was a busy day.

"What do you want for your birthday," I asked him some days ago. "You," he answered. He always says that. I thought of the trowel on my own, and had entertained vague thoughts of making him a nice dinner or taking him out somewhere in the evening. Something with a cake. Trowel and cake. Maybe the trowel stuck in the cake. Something.

But, instead, with no dinner and no trowel and no cake, we set out on foot with Grace from next door, carrying stubs of our old dinner candles in a bag. We walked to the train station, where the town has built a memorial to the 9/11 dead: a piazza with benches to sit on, a lovely public clock, brass plates with the names of everyone from New Jersey who died that day, with stars next to the ones from our town and the next town.

People milled around and talked quietly, holding up their candles against the gathering dark. An occasional train roared by. There were no speeches and no prayers. Q mingled and talked to people he didn't know, as he always does. At one point, he hopped to the top of a low wall, in order to hear a young man better. We did sing some songs: "*Dona Nobis Pacem*" and "Where Have All the Flowers Gone?" and many "Amens" at the end. We even sang "*La Marseillaise*," lifting our candles high on the "*Aux armes citoyens!*" One Democrat wanted to start a talk about the election of 2004, but the crowd wasn't there for that. We were there to share our fear and sorrow, to accompany one another in doing something when it seems there's not much left to be done.

Today is the day, we hear on the radio. Today there will be a regime change in Iraq, or a sudden laying down of arms there, or else our naval destroyers will begin traveling from the international waters off the coast of Turkey down to the Red Sea. This is approximately a two-day trip. When they arrive, the invasion will begin, I guess. This information sits in our stomachs like lead.

We stayed at the memorial until 8 P.M., when it was time to pass the vigil on to the next time zone. Then we walked on down Main Street toward home. But maybe it was time for a birthday dinner after all, a different one than I had imagined: one at the Thai place, one with fried rice in a pineapple and hot chilis and other things I don't know how to cook. One with no cake, but a special Thai pumpkin custard for the birthday boy.

When we got home, he went back to the Internet. Trying to decide whether he could squeeze in the time to go to the veterans' vigil in Washington.

Citizen Q. A man who reads the newspapers and worries about what he reads, and who also frets over the deterioration in punctuation he sees there. A man who loves his country and served it willingly more than fifty years ago. A man who drives carless people to the polls on election day. A joyous donor of blood. A man who sings "*La Marseillaise*" *tout en français* when other people are throwing out perfectly good French wine, a man who easily chooses a candlelight vigil over a cake. A citizen for seventy-five years.

New Prayers

We decided to eat dinner in front of the television so we could watch the president. We almost never watch the president, or anybody else—our news comes from radio. But there are times when you want to see.

Fifteen minutes. He had finished before we reached dessert. Q sliced our pears into delicious, juicy quarters. We ate them as the commentators piled on. Then they ran a program about the career of Saddam Hussein. Not an Eagle Scout, Saddam.

By the time I arose this morning, two cabinet ministers had resigned from under Tony Blair. I knew it already: I had slept with the BBC, so I could keep track of things in my sleep. This made me dream unsettling things: I was with a crowd in a burning building, pointed out the fact that the roof was made of wood, that the flames were reaching it. Then I was on a train, cleaning up someone else's trash that had been left on the seat.

This is one of those milestones in history. One of those events by which we mark time: *Let's see, now, that was before my mother died.... Let's see, that was before Madeline was born.... Let's see, that must have been during the war....* Who is to say how we will remember what is about to happen? But remember it we will. We'll bookmark our own biographies with it.

It is bigger than we are, and we will not be its decision-makers. So what *can* we do? We, who were powerless to prevent it?

We can pray. When someone says that, it's usually another way of saying that a situation is hopeless. *All we can do is pray*, as if that really weren't much. But it is. In fact, it's really *always* all we can do: the arrangements we make in the world are contingent at best. Our power doesn't count for much, and it vanishes in a puff of smoke. We give it everything we've got in the service of something we hold dear, but we do not manage its end. Before, during, and after we have worked as hard as we could, all we can do is pray.

I've been praying for the leaders of the world since forever. Been praying especially hard lately. Praying for the ones with whom I agree and the ones with whom I don't. Praying for the president and all his advisors. For all our soldiers and all of theirs. For all their children and ours. For their grandmothers, and ours. Praying for the United Nations. Praying for Saddam and for Osama, and everyone who looks to them. Don't think *that* hasn't been a challenge.

But it's what I can do. I can speak my mind and write a letter. I can make a donation and attend a vigil. I am one tiny voice, one little flame. With others, I became strong. But, perhaps, not many enough. We did not succeed in averting what is about to happen. Not everything in life succeeds. I knew that.

And now I must turn myself to a new reality, a new prayer. A sadder-but-wiser prayer. That what happens, happens quickly. That loss of life is minimal—ours and theirs. *Minimal,* I repeat, and a vision of one dead child reminds me how defeated a word "minimal" is. That, somewhere on the other side of all this, peace can take root and bloom. In my prayer, I watch God watching us.

Fools Rush In

I have taken the long way out to the car every morning since the crocuses first peeked above the ground a couple of weeks ago, and yesterday I was rewarded: flowers at last. Two whites, a yellow and two purples. And now the daffodil shoots are three and four inches tall, and the tulips are up. I pulled some of the heavy layer of mulch away from the garden in the front, and there were more daffodils, waiting for the sun. I planted a hundred bulbs last fall, and they have slept in the frozen earth all winter, and now it is time. This morning it is cold, but it won't matter. It will take more than a little chill to stop them now.

Hey, thanks for the flowers, I said to God. If ever I needed floral evidence of the inevitability of new life, it was on the day that we learned with sinking hearts of the inevitability of war. The earth felt good in my fingers as I tucked some leaf mold around a little daffodil. The sun shone warm on my back. The butterfly bushes reminded me that they would like to be pruned to the ground—and soon—and I told them I'll get to them tomorrow for sure.

My experiment with the canna lilies may or may not have worked. They are not supposed to be hardy in this climate zone, but I have spoken with many local gardeners who do leave theirs in the ground all winter, tucking them in with lots of mulch and covering them with evergreen boughs to keep them warm, and so I left mine in this year. This has worked well for folks around here during the mild winters of the recent past; will it work after this past winter's more orthodox, fierce cold? We'll just see.

I hope they don't die. If they do, it will have been at my hand. It will have been because I disregarded what we know about them, pushed them beyond their natural strength, demanded of them something they could not give. I look at them and don't feel very good about what I've done.

Today at noon I'll be preaching at Trinity Church, Wall Street. I'm doing three weeks and Roger Ferlo's doing three. We chatted weeks ago about titles for these sermons—reluctantly, for we both dislike sermon titles—and, not surprisingly, came up with the themes of fear and anxiety. So today, I'll be giving a sermon called "Fools Rush in Where Angels Fear to Tread," a title chosen long before we knew that we'll probably start bombing Iraq later this afternoon.

Perhaps I'll start with the canna lilies, with my cavalier treatment of them, my refusal to work with who they really are, with my insistence on bending them to my will. I will own up to being a colonial power where the cannas are concerned, not a gardener. A gardener assists plants in doing what they naturally do, provides them a place, offers them drinks and an occasional snack, treats them as equals. Gives them a nice warm bed, if that's what they need. Asks them what they need.

If the cannas make it, it won't be to my credit. I was interested in trying something new with them, so interested that I was willing to risk their lives. I did not approach these plants with the respect for their histories they deserve. Everybody deserves that.

If they make it, it will have been despite me. It will not have been my doing. It will have been by the grace of God.

The Old Story

"Decapitation" is the colorful but apt term for what happened last night. Or, rather what tried to happen: a precisely targeted strike at a specific person, the enemy's leader or leaders. Decapitation: to cut off the head. Someone had some good information as to Saddam's whereabouts, and some good information about how long he would be wherever he was. The brightest of our smart bombs would fly there, and he would be gone. Perhaps that would have been the last exchange of firepower in this war.

The decapitation almost worked, it seems. He almost was gone. A shaken but still blustering Saddam appeared on the television to demonstrate his continued existence, giving the date and time, just so we couldn't say it was a recording from an earlier time. He told his people several times to use their swords.

Whether they will or not remains to be seen: many think the people of Iraq are exhausted and discouraged, that little love is lost between them and their leader, that they may ponder their options and decide to choose life for themselves and their families, rather than death with the dictator. Some think that they will rejoice to see the Americans on the horizon, throw down their arms, and embrace a new future in fellowship with the rest of the world.

I certainly don't know what they will do. I have listened to some of them talk this way, and to others vow to fight to the end. Last night I heard an Iraqi businessman talk about the money to be made in Iraq after the war—a dealer in high-end jewelry, he was. The radio host thought it might be a while before emerald sales really pick up. Probably so.

People are making refugee camps on the borders with neighboring countries. We have refugee-camp kits now, you know: you just pop the top, and in an hour or two you have a little city for thousands of people. You can add to it easily if more people come.

Our prayers shift now. We pray for brevity and containment. We pray for the lives of those who do not decide but must participate. How many times in history has this happened, this shift in prayer? How many times have we had to shift our search for God in the midst of human trouble, shift from looking for God to get us out of what we have gotten into, to peering into the mess of it to find the little kernel of good that God draws from even the most devastating situation? It's in there somewhere, waiting for us to pick it up and look at it, for us to use it.

This is terrible. But God is very near to it, as is always so when terror comes.

O help us open our eyes to you, so we can see you and follow.

Wishful Thinking

I knew it was too early in the season, but, before I could help myself, I had soaked nine bean seeds in a cup of warm water for two hours, as you must do before you plant them. Now it was fish or cut bait: they either had to go in the ground somewhere or that was the end of them. But they need to be in ground that's warm. Like in late April or early May, not late March. So I put them into peat pots. The kitchen table is covered with peat pots, the window is full of them. They are everywhere. You can't eat on that table.

I spent a couple of happy hours both Saturday and Sunday in the warm sun, doing things too early: putting in sunflower seeds, planting nasturtiums. It's not too early to sprinkle poppy seeds, though, and I sprinkled with abandon: some in the rose barrel, some along the side of the house with the sunflowers-to-be.

For the most part, the things that go in too early will be fine: they'll just sit and pout until the soil warms to their liking, and then they will get busy, with no harm done. A sudden frost could end it all for some of them, but I have it in my mind that we won't have one. I always have this in my mind, every spring.

And there is usually a sudden frost.

I want something to be so, and so I expect that it will. I expect the best-case scenario. I am regularly informed by life that it does not always present itself, but I continue to expect it nonetheless.

We will roll into Iraq like a knife through warm butter. People will be thrilled to see us and welcome us with hugs and happiness. They have suffered under a dictator for too long, and they will cheer their liberators. Their dispirited soldiers will surrender immediately. We might take the whole country with barely a shot. This could be over in a matter of days.

Some did surrender—many hundreds, actually. Another band of soldiers came out with a white flag, and then ambushed those who came forward to receive their surrender. So now they have prisoners of war, as well. Friendly fire has claimed some victims. So did a terrible incident of fragging on our side—the killing of a military comrade. Once war is out of the box, its contradictory tentacles are everywhere, uncontrollable. This could be quick. This could be long. This could be anything.

Prayer expects the best. It cannot demand it, but it arises from hope and trust in a God who is good, and it expects to see goodness in the world, signs of that good God. Prayer is always puzzled and shocked by sorrow, as if it had never see it before. Should prayer become more realistic? Should it lower its sights, embrace more reasonable goals?

I think not. We force nothing into existence in our prayer, create nothing. God creates. And God hears, too: hears our longing. Our longing for the good is part of the world's history, just as much a part as someone else's terrible plans. And so we plant things too early, see them beautiful before they even arrive, imagine the best and pray for it. Without ever knowing for sure what will happen. It is not given us to know. But it is given us to hope.

Hardwired

"I thought they started singing at dawn," Q protested sleepily yesterday, when a bird began to chirp in the dark. No. They begin before dawn. They know it's coming before we do. They probably feel responsible for bringing it about. By the time the sun is actually up, they're raising an awful racket out there. More and more of them all the time, as the winter vacationers return.

Yesterday, What's-Her-Name spent an hour or so showing Gypsy the ropes, on one of their first joint ventures outside. Since Gypsy's surgery earlier this month, she's been confined to the house, but she's good to go now, and it's time for her to learn to hunt. What's-Her-Name is a fine hunter, and believes that, now that Gypsy's finished exploring her own sexuality, she should learn a trade.

Here's where you go in under the pine tree and hide, What's-Her-Name said, leading the way as Gypsy watched with interest from the picnic table. She slunk under the pine branches and began to climb—a superb climber, What's-Her-Name, although she has no claws in front. Soon she was at eye level with the bird feeder. I have known her to stay there all afternoon, watching.

And the birds watch. Most birds eat on the run. They look around, quickly pick up a seed and fly off with it to some safe place to eat it. They often station one of their number as a sentry, to sound the alarm if attack is imminent. In the end, the contest is all about speed: the ability to attack quickly, to flee quickly. Certain birds will dive-bomb a cat, in groups or even alone, if a baby is threatened. But most birds know they can't fight a cat and win. Mostly their goal is to get away.

Kate does not hunt. I don't believe it's because she's a pacifist: I have never known Kate to take a moral position. She just considers it beneath her. Instead, she begins howling for Q to fix her breakfast not long after the first bird has signaled the dawn, and her sorties into the garden are sybaritic: she wants a sun bath, or a bite or two of grass, or to sit in the shade and smell things, in a passive sort of cat aromatherapy. Kate is a consumer.

Not many birds meet an untimely end here, though—as good a hunter as What's-Her-Name is. Mostly it's mice, and we encounter their remains all the time.

She probably doesn't really have to teach Gypsy how to hunt. Gypsy was probably born knowing, or at least born knowing how to learn. Hardwired for hunting, cats. I wonder if we're hardwired for violence, too. We seem to be unable to go for long without a dose of it, unable to work things out in any other way. Unable to learn that war doesn't usually work things out.

Each generation has one war. At least one. Everybody hates it, but we keep doing it, and we have lived for so long within structures that demand it that we don't know any other way to live. We've long since institutionalized our own violence. We celebrate it, inserting it into places it doesn't belong: into our games, our lovemaking, our entertainment. Our inclusion of violence in these things—in everything—is so ancient that we can't imagine ourselves without it.

This morning, Gypsy and What's-Her-Name are engaged in a rousing game of Chase: up and down all three flights of stairs, as fast as they can run, turning up rugs and skidding around corners as they go. They do this over and over. It is great fun.

Kate blinks from her chair as they career past. She has never been like that. Hardwired for violence, maybe. But there are alternative temperaments in the cat world, as there are among us. There have always been nonviolent people. They're rarely in charge of anything, and conventional wisdom says that they're not up to it.

But think: Mohandas Ghandi. Martin Luther King. Aung San Suu Kyi. Changing their societies without violence. Maybe we don't under- stand what power is as clearly as we think we do. Maybe violence among us isn't an absolute given, the way we always shake our heads and say it is. Maybe it's a decision.

Maybe we could make a different one.

The Silver Herring

I found Q in the bathroom. He was wearing a face full of shaving soap and his Tigger boxer shorts, the gift of his grandsons. *Always give a gift you would like to receive yourself* is their motto.

"What should I write my eMo about?" I asked Q. I had tried some of my usual tricks to stimulate writing: sitting in my usual chair, reading Morning Prayer while the computer starts up, casting my mind back over odd thoughts that had come to me in my sleep. They usually prime the pump, but sometimes they don't.

Asking somebody is another trick. Q is a professor, though, and always wants his students to come up with their own ideas, so I rarely get a direct suggestion. I looked at the Tigger boxer shorts and decided against writing about them. I used the time to get dressed and curl my hair, so as not to look like the Witch of Endor at Trinity Church this noon. Sometimes doing something *else* helps the paralysis, although you don't want it to be too absorbing a task or you'll forget about the writing entirely. Something with an exit strategy, like getting dressed or doing your hair or making your bed. I made the bed. Then I came back into my office and sat down.

One thing that unlocks writing is reading work you've already written. Go over something you've finished and let yourself see how good it is. Make an editorial change here and there to make it even better. Before you know it, you're unfrozen, and can turn to the work at hand.

Q appeared with tea and toast. How lovely. I read him the above allusions to not writing about the Tigger boxer shorts. "If you don't want to use them, why are you mentioning them?" he asked. A reasonable, English-professor sort of question. "I want to set the scene," I said. "Let them see what a red herring looks like, if they don't know." He snorted, put down the teapot, and left.

You all probably know what a red herring looks like. To begin with, it doesn't exist. Herrings are a silvery grey. Hold out for a red one and you'll waste a lot of time—chasing something you can never have and in doing so, ignoring lots of things you can. And that's what a red herring looks like.

Time is getting short. Heaven is eternal, but life on earth is brief. We don't have an infinity of days left before us to do the things we are here to do. Blink your eyes and life is half over. Better figure out where you're supposed to be and get there. Learn to recognize the red herrings, so you can ignore them. Our red herrings are often other people's silver ones—we think we're supposed to do something because someone we admire does it. No. To each his or her own herring. Pursue your own.

When you're on the trail of what you are called to pursue, it flows. You may not have a fabulous day every day, but your work flows out of you in a powerful stream and you love that stream. You have the feeling of a good job well done. You want to focus on it, don't want to leave it, leave it only reluctantly, with a promise to be back, a promise that you keep. You don't wonder why you show up very day—you know why.

Is your work that? The silver herring? Or, if not your work, something? Your family and its needs? Everyone has one, a call that asserts itself insistently and repeatedly. A fish you can catch. Wade in the water and grab it, while you still can.

A Good Breakfast

We have two kinds of oatmeal: Quaker and Irish. Quaker is for oatmeal raisin cookies and for when I only have ten minutes to cook it—there are times when I have oatmeal for supper, if I am alone, and it's usually Quaker.

But Irish is real oatmeal. It comes in a tin, like a coffee tin, and your first hint that you're not in Kansas is when you open it up and look inside: no soft uniform flakes. Instead, hard pellets of oats with the hulls still on is what you get with Irish. You have to cook it for about half an hour, or you could break a tooth. You put raisins in it at the end of cooking, if you like raisins. Q adds buttermilk at this point. "Stay away from mine with that buttermilk," I remind him.

This morning, Q is downstairs making Irish. The hulls have just now softened enough to burst open, and the smell they release is heavenly. It reminds me of my father, of mornings at our house when I was a girl. When my grandmother was dying, I was convinced that she would get strong again if I fed her oatmeal, and I would fill a nice tray with a breakfast she probably could scarcely bear to look at. How she found the strength to thank me so kindly every day, I cannot now imagine.

Q appears at the door to my office with a fragrant bowl of oatmeal and a lovely cup of tea. How absolutely lovely. The sun comes through the window and the birds are at the feeder—we are all having grain.

I am listening to the news. The sun is shining in Iraq, too: the sandstorm is over, and it is late afternoon. There are hours of light, enough time to fight again. Soon it will be night, and there will be cover in which to bomb, in which to peer through the darkness with our infrared scopes. And tomorrow, everyone will need a good breakfast. Soldiers eat a lot. Contrary to popular legend, the food is usually pretty good, and there's a lot of it.

The children of Basra will awaken hungry, too. A good breakfast is important for growing children—the most important meal of the day, my mother always used to say. I imagine the mothers of Basra believe this, too: all mothers believe it. Cooking breakfast is going to be tough this morning: they're running out of water. Running out of food, too, soon. Humanitarian aid can't get through yet, and Red Cross engineers have not been given access to repair the water-delivery system.

The tea is hot and sweet in my mouth, and the oatmeal was delicious. Now my stomach is pleasantly full. The soldiers will have their breakfast soon—maybe oatmeal, for those who want it. Those out on patrol will eat some strange things, nothing hot and wonderful like my breakfast, but enough to keep them going.

It's the children of Basra who concern me.

The Gift of Fire

"Can you manage that?" Q asked, as I attempted to lift a log as big around as I am. No, I couldn't, but I could knock it off the pile and roll it over to the log splitter. Then I could roll it up the side of the splitter and position it onto the track. All without actually lifting it. This is how primitive people discovered escalators.

The log splitter is kind of like a slow guillotine: it pushes the log along a track into the edge of a blade, which splits it in half. You've seen them in silent movies, in which the damsel in distress is tied up on one, screeching her way along the track, saved by the hero—in the nick of time—from being split in half.

We were splitting two cords of wood, easy. Maybe three. We got it free last summer, when two nice young men offered it to us and then piled it five feet high in our driveway, blocking the sun from the vegetable garden. I guess nothing in life is really free.

Did we want to cancel the log splitter for the afternoon? the rental guy had asked on the answering machine. Looks like rain. We looked at each other. I'm in Texas next Saturday and somewhere else the Saturday after that. Rain or no rain, we had to seize the day.

And the rain held off, for the most part. It took us four hours to split sixty or seventy immense logs into hundreds of smaller, burnable ones. We took turns, one on the controls (easy) and one bringing the next log (*not* easy). I rolled most of them, when it was my turn to do the hard part; Q carried his. Showoff. And, at the end of our labors, after the last log blew apart like a shot and fell into two symmetrical halves, we were surrounded by a log house as tall as we were. Enough for two years. Maybe three. As the rain finally fell, we shook hands like the partners we were. "We're a good team," I said, and he nodded.

We told Gwen and Tom about our feat in the Indian restaurant afterwards. "We'll regret this tomorrow," we said. "Maybe not tomorrow," Gwen said, "but maybe Monday." Gwen knows her orthopedics, having traded in a hip for a newer model some years ago.

And now today is Monday. Not too bad. I can certainly feel it, but I can move. Q bounds out of bed and down the stairs, as usual. We still need to move the pile to its permanent resting place, and I'm not sure where that will be. It used to be next to the house, and a possum lived in it. We would see him at night, sometimes, coming home late. That was before we had the hunting cat What's-Her-Name, whom no possum could hope to outrun.

We don't need the logs to heat our house: we have a furnace. Q says using the fireplace actually reduces the heat in the house—it goes up the chimney, he says, and you're better off without it. There's more to life than physics, though. There's the hypnotic sight of flames licking a log while you stare and stare, the crackle of the wood punctuating quiet talk. There's the comforting glow of a fire in the dark, and the kiss of warmth, just enough, in the early fall before you turn the heat on in the house. Worth a few aches and pains the day after splitting a few hundred logs.

The gift of fire to humanity was an important one. In Greek mythology, it was Prometheus who brought it to us, a Titan who stole it from the gods and brought it down. They didn't want us to have it, and punished Prometheus for his action: he had to be tied to a rock and have buzzards come and eat his liver out every night for the rest of time. Those Greeks sure held a grudge.

The Promethean fire was not evil. It was mixed. It was a gift: we could do good things with it, like cook, and make bricks, and stay warm in the winter, and clear land quickly. But it was a two-edged gift: fire destroys as well.

We don't have a fire myth in our tradition. We have Adam and Eve, upon whom we blame all the evil in the world, but fire is not mentioned in the Garden of Eden, until they are expelled from it: then the cherubim stationed at the eastern entrance to guard against their return are accompanied by a fiery sword, which seems to flash back and forth in front of the gate more or less on its own.

And then the fire that was absent from the lost garden of our first parents became the primary vehicle of sacrifice to the God who banished them: the flesh of animals and offerings of grain, set upon stone altars and burned, sending fragrant smoke toward heaven to delight the Almighty. Why they thought God liked all that smoke is lost in the mists of time.

Yesterday, thousands of small fires went out all over New York: no more smoking in bars. No smoking in bars? Impossible! Nobody will go to them if they can't smoke. But I'm sure they will—San Francisco bars have been smoke-free for some time, yet people still go. How people started to smoke is as lost in history as why people used to burn animals to God: *How about I roll these leaves up in a larger leaf and light one end? Then I think I'll put the other end in my mouth and suck in the smoke really hard. That'll probably be good.*

But even this irrational, harmful habit is mixed. Smoking calms them. They feel convivial when they're holding a cigarette, and it gives them something to do with their hands. It may be deadly. But it is not without its benefits.

There's not a good thing in the world that can't be misused. You can take every gift God gives humanity and ruin it: you can use sex for violent ends, abuse trust, pervert learning, manipulate love of country, decimate the natural environment and all its living things.

But God showed himself to Moses in fire first: a fire that burned, but did not destroy. A fire whose destructive power was canceled by the divine love. When the bombs drop, they leave things in flame. We have watched Baghdad in flames night after night—destructive fire. Where now is the fire that burns but does not destroy?

Come speedily and save us, O God. Save those who burn and those who send fire to the earth. Come and turn history, and bring life out of death again.

Something Happened

There's a procedure: you fire some warning shots into the air and the vehicle is supposed to stop. If it doesn't, you stop it by firing at it. The carnage of the first few suicide car bombings makes this all a little easier to contemplate, but it doesn't make it easier to do. And yesterday, a terrible mistake: the driver didn't heed the warning shot, maybe didn't understand what it meant, maybe the warning shots didn't come quickly enough, something—and when the passenger section of the van was opened, the worst: all women and children. All dead.

The investigation is still going on. It could actually have been an attempted suicide bombing—they use human shields. Or it could have been a simple case of the driver's panicking at the first shot and trying to get away. Who would not do the same? Nobody knows yet what happened. Nobody may ever know.

Amadou Dialo reached into his pocket for his wallet, so he could show his ID. He didn't have a gun; the cops were nervous, and thought he did. With a fraction of a second to study the situation, they came to a mistaken conclusion. They fired. There were forty-one bullet holes in his body.

Why do we have nothing to fear but fear itself? Because fear is what kills. More than anything else. It anticipates harm and either runs for cover or strikes first. Its anticipation of harm may be well-founded or it may not be, but harm is in the air, sucked into the soul with every breath. And you never know, until it's too late. You cannot know until afterward, and yet must act now.

And then, open the car door and see the dead, and know that it was your bullets, and know that you will see this every time you close your eyes for the rest of your life, that your children will never know what it was to see it, will never understand how it pierces every vision you will ever have of their smiles. Lie awake and try to rewind this terrible tape, make it unhappen. Try to unshoot. Walk backwards, away from the car, and keep walking backwards, miles and miles, walk backwards over the sea to your home, all the way back to when you were a kid, before any of this happened.

They know not what they do. Not until afterward, when it cannot be undone. *Bless them. They did not ask to be there, to do this. And bless them: they were only trying to get away. Bless them all.*

Prayer Makes Us Part of God's Work

"I don't watch at all anymore," my friend says. "I was doing nothing else, just glued to the television, watching those explosions over and over. I don't even want to talk about it."

How long can you watch something that looks and sounds like the Fourth of July but isn't? Feel yourself rocked with each flash and the terrible BOOM that follows it, hoping that this bomb was as smart as all the others? We have limits.

But don't boycott the news altogether. Don't retreat into your shell until it's over. Just force yourself to do something else most of the day, and most of your available time off. Your work should take care of forty-plus hours of it, since they probably don't let you watch CNN all day there. And your leisure time should be that: in the garden, or reading a book, or at the gym, in the park, hearing music, out to dinner with a friend. It's important for us to remember why it is that we think life is good. And most of our lives are good because of the little things we have in them. The ordinary things.

We need to balance ourselves. God has business for us concerning the war, and overdosing on it—so that we can no longer bear to think about it at all—makes us unavailable for whatever that business might be. Unavailable and worse, perhaps. Hostile to the healing that needs to happen among us.

Thirty years ago we were too conflicted about the Vietnam War to offer any comfort and kindness to our returning American soldiers. Let's not do that again. We need to pray now, and pray with an open heart, not an exhausted, defensive one. The great river of God's love flows all around this situation, touching each man, woman, and child affected. Our little trickle of love enters that mighty stream when we pray, and we are in line with it, carried along with its great power. Thus, we relate to people we will never meet in prayer, people on both sides. And it changes us. And, in ways we will never know, it changes them.

Well, can't God just work in them without our prayers, and leave us out of it? Of course. But we wouldn't be part of the work, wouldn't be in the river of God's love. We'd be standing on the riverbank, wringing our hands, or standing there with our backs turned, pretending nothing was happening. We would have sat this one out, while other people gave their lives believing we were worth dying for.

This will not last forever. It will be over. Soon, soon, we pray. But whenever it is over, those who can reconcile will be called upon to do so, and to lead others in doing so. Those who have prayed constantly will be united to friend and foe alike, in a new way ready to be led into a new relationship. In Christ, war is never really about winning, though each side desperately wants to win. Christ works for the end of war, pushes past the failure of human efforts at peace to the time when it is over, looks forward to the unknowable peace he already holds in his hand, waiting to give it out to all of us.

The Meaning of God

Then a voice came from heaven.... The crowd standing there heard it and said that it was thunder. Others said, "An angel has spoken to him."

John 12:28–29

If you're over five years old, you've probably already realized that we don't always know how to recognize the voice of God. Sometimes I understand only after the fact that God has spoken to me. Sometimes I never get it on my own, and someone else has to tell me.

God transmits faithfully. I just don't receive very well.

"There *is* a God," somebody says when a parking place opens up right in front of the place where he's going. Everybody in the car laughs. God certainly speaks in the good things that happen to us, large and small, and we recognize the voice. We're confident enough to joke about it.

The voice of God in the other things, the harder things, is harder to hear. *This can't be God,* we think, *I'm in too much pain.* And, on some level, we are correct: God isn't *causing* our pain. God doesn't just cause things; God *means* things. It's not true that the only way God can be present in a situation is if God caused it. The presence of God is way more complicated than that. And, at the same time, much simpler.

When Joseph is sold into slavery by his jealous brothers, we're not told that this is God's will. That it was God's idea. That God did it. It was a rotten thing to do. People did it, not God, and the people who did it were behaving abominably. It inaugurated a long and colorful story of God's providence, though, all through Joseph's life and into the Exodus. "You meant it for ill," a generous Joseph told his remorseful brothers when all was forgiven, "but God meant it for good."

God *means* things.

God brings good out of evil. Evil doesn't stop being evil because God brings good out of it—it's still evil. We don't have to tap-dance feverishly around painful history until we can come up with a way to say it's really not painful. Life can be terribly painful. Bad things are still bad. But God can mean them for good. Give them meaning they didn't have. Give them more than one meaning. Use them as platforms for healing and deliverance, beyond what any of us could ask or imagine.

We all get a chance to let God "mean" things in life. Usually, we get many chances: life is hard. We stumble and fall, or something crashes into us and knocks us to the ground. *This is terrible,* we think. And, indeed, it is. The next few chapters are God's writing, though: the way in which the spirit struggles to search and find, falls silent and accepts healing, peers into the abyss and sees a glimmer of light.

The voice of God that Jesus hears in this Sunday's Gospel is a prediction of his death. Not much good to be said about what goes on in that story, which we all know so well: betrayal, mob violence, travesties of justice and religion. Not much good until God "means" it, and then we know it to be the beginning of the story of resurrection.

These are terrible times. The news is hard, and the death of young people tears at our hearts. Not much good to be said about all this. But stay tuned. It is at just such times—terrible times, times when death is rampant and evil runs loose—that God steps forward and begins the task of helping us sift through the tragedy and find meaning: almost never in the cause of our pain, but in what can happen among us because of it.

The Gospel reading for the Fifth Sunday in Lent, Year B, is John 12:20–33.

The Flower of Home

"I'd love to see them," I said. The Texan had been telling me about the fields of bluebonnets not two miles from where we were standing. I had to see them to believe them, he said. He said that Texans feel about their bluebonnets the way the Japanese feel about their cherry blossoms—not just that they are lovely flowers, but that the flowers are actually a part of them. "Part of our souls," he said.

"I'd love to see them," I said again.

"Got fifteen minutes?" he asked, and we were off.

The first few bluebonnets appeared alongside the road, drifts of deep blue, interspersed with the bright orange of Indian paintbrush.

Then, through the trees, a sight that made me gasp out loud: a whole field of bluebonnets, bluer than any flower I've ever seen, striped through here and there with slashes of orange.

"Like a Persian carpet," the Texan said. Yup. Just like that.

"This is unbelievable," I said, and it was just that. I had seen pictures of bluebonnets in garish calendars and thought them retouched. No. They really are just that lovely. I got out of the car and stepped into the midst of the flowers. I knelt down and smelled them. Sweet, a little spicy. The flower of the Texan soul.

Part of the Texan soul: a flower. And of the Japanese soul: a flower. And the rows of crosses in Flanders fields are interspersed right now with nodding red poppies, happy and hopeful against the green grass and the white marble. "This is a beautiful country," my friend wrote back from Afghanistan, "absolutely beautiful. Right now I'm looking at a field of wildflowers."

The sky over Iraq is black, and nobody has much time right now to look for flowers in its desert. The heat rises every day, and we think it must suck all the green life from the landscape. But there is life that lives there, green that can survive it. Not our kinds of plants. Their own kind. Plants we don't know about.

There is probably a flower that is part of the Iraqi soul. I don't know what it is. It's not a Texas bluebonnet. It's probably not a poppy. But there is a flower that an Iraqi sees with a pleasure deeper than just the appreciation of beauty. This is the flower of home.

Someday this war will be over. The people will plant gardens again, and harvest fruit. They will pick flowers again, and sell them in the cities that now are pitted with the craters of bombs, smudged with the smoke of them. The rest of the world will have to help them rebuild those cities, but we will not supply them with all their seeds. They will need to use their own seeds. Seeds for their land, for plants that will grow and flourish there. Seeds of their own beauty.

Would you like to see? one of them will say when we visit, in peaceful years to come. *Got fifteen minutes?*

The Danger of Success

I was lazy this morning, Monday in Holy Week, my first day back at the eMo mill since my return from Texas. I have had much of which to complain since my return—always a pleasure. There has been my painfully swollen leg to whine about, and a few basil seedlings, who did not survive my absence. I carried a pottery oil lamp back home with me and broke its handle in transit, and now I'll have to glue it. A tulip was smashed into oblivion by a falling slate tile from the roof.

But the war is over.

Or maybe it is not. "Nobody has told us it's finished," a young soldier told an interviewer. He and his colleagues stand uneasily around Baghdad, guarding things. They're not policemen, and they don't take to it. Looters sack the hospitals, break into the museum and walk off with the archaeological heritage of most of the fertile crescent, smashing priceless ancient urns on the streets, carrying off irreplaceable gold and silver objects to melt them down and sell the metal, and nobody stops them. Other people want to come close to the soldiers, to shake their hands, to give them a flower. They don't allow it. *Maybe one of these people is a suicide bomber,* they think. Maybe. They've intercepted two already.

President Bush mentions, as if in passing, that Syria may have weapons of mass destruction. Tell me I didn't hear him say that.

Yesterday we waved palm branches in the air and welcomed Jesus into Jerusalem. He'll be dead by Friday afternoon. Public opinion is a fickle thing. People expect you to deliver quickly.

We should remember that.

Our soldiers may be coming home soon.

The cost of the war was reassuringly modest.

Our POWs are safe.

Good.

But many people opposed the war to begin with, for reasons that have not changed. Our military victory ought to have surprised no one—we're huge and Saddam was weak. Of course we won. But what now?

Syria? Maybe Iran? Why not Libya, while we're in the neighborhood? Today on the radio, I heard a woman talk about the entire Middle East as having attacked us on 9/11. That's not my memory of it.

Our thinking should not be clouded because we love and respect our sons and daughters, and long for their safe return. We still must do the work of peace, and war is an odd place to begin it. We still must examine ourselves and our posture within the world community, and the flush of victory will make it hard to do that. But every reason why it was important to look at ourselves six months ago still exists today. And there's nobody on earth—no nation and no individual—who doesn't need to conduct a daily examination of conscience. Such a thing comes more easily to losers—*where did we go wrong?* But winners have a harder time being honest with themselves. It looks to them as if history has certified their rightness. But be careful. We're never in greater spiritual danger than we are when we have triumphed.

Life, Death, and Taxes

It was hot and airless in the post office lobby, which was too small for the line of people snaking around it. I was hoping the workers behind the windows were air-conditioned and more comfortable: I had just heard one of them say that it was the worst Monday he'd ever seen, and I didn't want any of them to crack under the strain.

There is no reason to have a large lobby in our post office. Metuchen is a small town, and you don't usually meet more than one or two people coming in or going out. Except right now. *Everyone* was there yesterday, except for those who are there today, mailing off our tax forms. We were all rendering unto Caesar.

Caesar said yesterday that he thought our taxes were too high. He always says that. I don't agree with him. I think it's an honor to pay them. Even when I disagree with what we're doing with the money, which I often do. I think it's adult to pay them, and not to expect something for nothing. I think that it's a duty to care for those less fortunate than I am, including those who don't have the sense to plan ahead for their own good; and I think that sometimes government is the one to do that. I think it's a privilege to live in a country where you can disagree with the president and not be afraid of a knock on your door. That's worth standing in line in an airless post office lobby for, any day.

But it was nice, finally, to mail the fat envelopes and step outside. Yesterday was beautiful here: blue sky with not a cloud, bright sun. Flowers everywhere.

Everywhere, including in a pile beside our front door. Speaking of people without the sense to plan ahead, I seem to have ordered twice the number of dahlias and hollyhocks that I needed. I believe I forgot the first order and then did it all over again. And I understand some special blue geraniums that I also forgot about are on their way.

Well, we'll make room. Frances is coming down to the Geranium Farm—she is in the mood to dig in the earth, but lives in an apartment, where it probably wouldn't be a good idea to do that.

We'll continue our work on the garden in front, where more ivy needs to be removed and compost dug in. The earthworms have been busy in the compost pile all winter, in an orgy of digestion, which will by now have produced something dark and wonderful at the bottom of the pile. We will wonder together whether or not I have killed the canna lilies—it is still too soon to tell.

The crocuses are finally up, Genevra writes. She is in Wellsville, New York, way upstate and west, where snow lingers a lot longer than it does down here. They're just now getting their crocuses, when ours are just about gone and the crocuses of Georgia have been gone for a month and a half. They may have to wait for them up there, but eventually the flowers come.

Death and taxes—those are the only two things you can count on, they say. But I think there are three: life, death, and taxes. You wouldn't have death if you didn't have life. The plants come up every year, more and more every year. Some of them don't—maybe the cannas won't, and maybe it'll be my fault. But others will. And *we're* still here.

Open Minds

I look up from my teacup and start a bit: What's-Her-Name is looking back at me through the window. She is sitting in the window box. "What are you doing there?" I ask her through the glass. She looks at me without blinking and does not move.

Maybe she wants to come inside. I go to the back door and open it invitingly. I call her in a nice voice. She doesn't move. She isn't sitting in the window box to get my attention. She's just spying on us.

From the window box, she can keep an eye on things inside and also on the bird feeder outside. The birds don't seem to mind—I think they, too, like to have What's-Her-Name out in the open, where they can see her. But I mind: I have tiny nasturtium and petunia seedlings in the window box, and they won't grow with a furry cat sitting on them. Moreover, the window box may suggest itself to What's-Her-Name as a personal latrine, and that's no good.

I am trying to understand What's-Her-Name in hopes that I can head off some of her more troublesome behaviors. I bought a book called *Pawmistry*, on how to read the paws of cats, the way people read human palms. You can tell from the pads on their feet what their personalities are, it says in the book, and you can tell from the bumps on their heads whether or not they love you. I think we already know the answer to that: cats are in it for themselves.

I can't tell if *Pawmistry* is satire or on the level. I got it at my acupuncturist's office, where you can also buy organic scones made with filtered water and organic cranberries and a dozen different whole grains. Everyone there is pretty earnest and very sweet, just the sort of people you would want sticking a host of tiny needles into you if you wanted to be stuck with tiny needles. I'm not sure satire is on their menu.

So I think somebody thinks you can read a cat's paw and do a cat's horoscope. Good Lord.

But then, I never would have believed ten or twenty little needles inserted in strategic mysterious places would have much to do with making my arthritic knees hurt less, and they do. Honest. A placebo? Maybe—if so, I don't care; I'm in it for the pain relief.

We should be more open-minded than we usually are. More open to mystery. Maybe you really *can* read a cat's paw and do its horoscope. Maybe not. Maybe I won't catch one of ours tonight and see.

Easter People

"If I can just make it through Easter," the exhausted priest tells me.

"Will you get some time off?" I ask. He is not the rector; he is the assistant. Usually the rector takes off after Easter, and the assistant has to wait. The church can be a hierarchical place.

"Monday," he says, brightening just a little. "And Tuesday."

"What are you going to do?"

He's thinking of going to a monastery. Or maybe he'll just work in his garden—he hasn't quite decided. Something that will soothe and delight him. This afternoon, he says, he's going to try to grab a nap. That sounds like a good idea. But there are sermons to write, still, and rehearsals of liturgies. And still, the stuff of parish life: people in hospitals, people in mourning, people who need him.

For us, the Three Days that begin today on Maundy Thursday are an intense story in which it all comes together, sometime in the night on Saturday, when Jesus crosses over from death to life. We know how it ends. Over the centuries, it has become an ornate dance, a dance of liturgy, of flowers, of shining brass and silver, of a sudden small fire in the night and candlelight spreading throughout the darkened church, of an even more sudden burst of light and singing, bells. For us, it is large crowds of people we do not ordinarily see, women in wonderful hats, children in new dresses, little boys in tiny blue blazers, proud and uncomfortable in their first ties.

But for those who first lived them, these three days were not about anything coming together. They were about things coming apart. Things going terribly wrong. Dashed hopes. Anger and betrayal. Jesus crossed from death to life, all right, but it took a long time for people to know it. Even his closest people. All they saw was all we see: loss and fear.

Take care of each other when I am gone, he tells his friends, *you're going to need one another,* and he shows them how: he performs a menial task of grooming, washing their dusty feet himself. He shares a lovely meal with them. He shows them how every meal from then on will contain him, if they will see it that way. And they begin the process we continue: the lifelong task of being faithful when faith seems unrewarded. If there is anyone left who still thinks that faith means life is going to be an unchallenged walk into inevitable success and daily pleasure, that person just hasn't been paying attention.

"We're supposed to be Easter people," the priest says, disappointed in himself. "We're supposed to show forth calm and hope no matter what." As if he's never supposed to be weary or dispirited. As if he's not allowed.

We may be Easter people, but we're not the damn Easter Bunny. God chooses to work through actual human beings, not magical paragons of strength and perfection. Jesus rises from the dead with his wounds clearly visible—it is how people recognize him. Through the wounds and one other way—handing out bread in a communal meal. It's all in how you allow yourself to see the meal. And the wounds.

Easter Even

I was jerked awake by a thought: I could dye all our Easter eggs red, using beet juice. I could do this today, when I am also going to remove the ivy from the front garden and plant about thirty perennials, make the summer pudding for tomorrow's dinner, mix the dough for the rolls, set the table, put up the curtain that the cats tore down, conduct a premarital counseling appointment, and get my roots touched up so I don't look like a skunk when I celebrate the Easter Vigil this evening.

I lay very still, and the thought passed. That was a close one.

But I *could* dye eggs with beet juice. I could even take a little flower from the garden—the vinca is flowering right now, and it's just the right size—dip it into melted wax and affix it to the egg.

Then, when I colored the egg, the flower would remain white.

This thought *hasn't* passed, and the beet juice is back. Maybe I'll do the ivy another day.

You only get to dye Easter eggs once a year. Is there anything like the smell of hot vinegar in the little bowls, the blossoming of the tablets of dye into yellow and blue and red and purple and green? Is there anything better than dipping your first egg into the color and lifting it immediately, to see that it is already a pastel version of its future self?

No, there isn't. And today is the day. This Easter, we're going beet.

Q is a devotee of the beet, and a child of the Great Depression, so we always save all the cooking liquid from vegetables. I make him save the beet liquid separately: its color is ... well, *assertive.* We always have beet juice on hand. It doesn't get used up as fast as the others. Not everyone wants to eat purple rice.

What other foods could I use to dye eggs with? Tea, of course: my grandmother used to do that. Not very bright, though, those tea-dyed eggs. Asparagus colors the water a pale chartreuse, and we had asparagus last week, so there's probably some in the refrigerator. I think of beet red and chartreuse eggs together in a bowl, though, and my mind misgives: we'll stick with beet. It'll match the red dining room.

And I'll get to the other things eventually. The dinner things first. The church things, of course. The hair is a must: it's looking pretty scary. But first, the eggs. Bright red. My grandmother used to rub them with a little butter to make them shiny. If you soak a hard-boiled egg in vinegar overnight, its shell turns soft and weird: this is very interesting, and kids like it. Or, if you don't want to live on hard-boiled eggs all week, you can make a quarter-inch hole in each end with a needle, blow out the contents into a bowl and have omelets for the rest of your life.

We used to have our Easter egg hunt in the graveyard at church when I was little. We swarmed over the graves, among the old tombstones tilting at crazy angles, our voices chirping in the quiet of that silent city. I was too young to consider the poetry of our presence there, the descent of loud young life upon the place of the dead, the hunt for brightly colored symbols of new life in the tomb. Our parents must have thought about it, though. It was as if death really were vanquished there, on those Easter mornings long ago. And I guess it really was. He is not here. He is risen.

Company for Dinner

"Is Lee really dead?" I asked PJ, as we sat around after Easter dinner. "Somehow it just doesn't seem right." We had just watched a video of her last show, in which she sang a song that Lee had never liked and made a joke about being free to sing it now. The audience laughed. We laughed.

New Yorkers who lost people during the year before the World Trade Center bombing got shortchanged a bit in their grief process. It takes about a year for their absence to begin to sink in, really, and people need time to learn to live in the new way and space to do it in. But Lee's year was cut short: we were too busy with the terrible aftermath of the larger tragedy, too distressed and absorbed, too frightened about future attacks. The first anniversary of his death passed in a blur of other obituaries, of funerals and bomb scares and sirens.

Everybody agreed. Something about Lee's death just seems ... unlikely. We haven't seen him in a while, it's true, but it continues to feel as if he might be in a road company, somewhere, the tenor in yet another barbershop quartet in yet another production of *The Music Man*, on the bus from one Midwestern city to another.

There's a man in the neighborhood who looks like Lee, and even walks like him. "I stay away from him," PJ says. "My heart stops when I look up and see him coming toward me. It's just too weird."

But he is gone. Gone from among us. One of his beloved cats is gone, too, now, PJ tells me. Lee named his cats after great actors and actresses. I think it was Olivia de Havilland who died, but I'm not sure. It might have been Maggie the Cat. I think Errol Flynn was already dead, but it could have been Errol Flynn.

Lee would have liked the dinner. He would have loved the summer pudding we had for dessert, I think, and would have appreciated its richness, astounding in view of its being low in sugar and fat free. He would have talked about opera and musicals all during dinner. He would have watched the videotape of her show, and he would have criticized the performance to within an inch of its life.

But then, who is to say the dead *don't* watch? Because we can't apprehend them doesn't mean they don't apprehend *us*. Perhaps the risen life is all around us, even now. When Jesus talked about the Kingdom of God, he always used the present tense: *The Kingdom of God is like this, and that, and this....* Something happened on that first Easter morning so long ago, something that so puzzled and shocked those who experienced it that they couldn't agree on what it was. Some of them were so confused they said nothing to anybody. Maybe it wasn't a return to life as we know it, but it was a return to some kind of life. Risen life. Christ gone before us, so we could all follow.

And that's how they live now. That risen life, a life we don't understand. Jesus often compared it to a banquet. If it is like that, I imagine the food is all like the summer pudding we had yesterday: rich and delicious and gorgeous—and fat free.

Summer Pudding

1 quart fresh strawberries
1 pint blueberries
$1/2$ pint raspberries

Place all the strawberries and almost all the other berries, leaving a few out for garnish, into a large sauce pot. Add about a cup of water and about a cup of Splenda (you can use real sugar, but why would you?). Bring to a boil and cook for 15–20 minutes. Remove from heat.

Cover bottom of a large-ish casserole, soufflé dish, or ring mold with a layer of the mixture, and cover that with a layer of sliced white bread from which you either have or have not removed the crusts.

Continue to layer the fruit mixture with the bread slices until both are gone. Cover with plastic wrap and set a china plate on top of the plastic. Place in refrigerator, putting a heavy can of something on top to weight it down. Leave it there for about eight hours.

To serve, unmold by slipping a knife all around the edge to loosen pudding. Invert your serving plate on top of the pudding—it should either be a bit larger in diameter than the pudding or have a lip, so your table cloth doesn't get fruit stains on it—and, holding the two dishes together with your opposable thumbs (if you have them), turn the whole thing upside down and carefully set the serving dish down with the now-inverted pudding on top. Tap it smartly all over its bottom, and it will slip safely onto the plate. If it doesn't, wait awhile, and it will eventually. Carefully lift off the pudding pan and sigh with pleasure. Garnish with the reserved berries and some mint if you have any, and serve with or without sweetened, nonfat sour cream (1 pint nonfat sour cream mixed with ¼ cup Splenda or sugar).

Nine people can have second and even third helpings of this dish, and the cook will still have a spoonful or two to eat while she does the dishes. *Bon appetit.*